I0644515

South Fukien
Missionary Poems
1925 –1951

South Fukien
Missionary Poems
1925 –1951

William Angus

Edited with an Introduction by

David Andrews

Foreword by

David Angus

MerwinAsia
Portland, Maine

MERWIN
ASIA

Copyright ©2015 by MerwinAsia
All rights reserved.

No part of this book may be reproduced in any form without written permission from the publisher, MerwinAsia,
59 West St., Unit 3W,
Portland, ME 04102
USA

www.merwinasia.com

Distributed by the University of Hawai'i Press

Library of Congress Control Number: 2014940600

ISBN 978-1-937385-55-2 (pbk)
ISBN 978-1-937385-56-9 (cloth)

Printed in the United States of America

The paper used in this publication meets the minimum requirements of the American National Standard for Information Services—Permanence of Paper for Printed Library Materials, ANSI/NISO Z39/48-1992

And He from one made every race of man

To live upon the face of the whole earth,

And of their epochs He has fixed the span

And set the limits of their going forth . . .

—William Angus,
from "Paul Before the Areopagus" (Acts 17:26)

Contents

FOREWORD

It is difficult to explain the realities of missionary life in the field to readers who may be acquainted only with the general geography of a foreign nation, or with stereotypical photos of displaced Midwesterners in pith helmets and puttees, squinting into the camera through thick spectacles. China, in particular, evokes exotic images of an ancient civilization with deep cultural foundations, and a fluctuating history punctuated by ferocious wars alternating with eras of peace and stability dedicated to the cultivation of philosophy, horticulture, and the arts. The truth, however, is at the same instant more prosaic—and more poetic.

Those American missionaries who ventured into China, especially between the years of 1842 through 1951, confident that they would serve as doctors, nurses, teachers, and evangelists to the heathen, were themselves irresistibly converted into learners, listeners to the pulse and rhythms of the people and to the great story that is China itself. In those days when radios were scarce and film entertainment available only in cities with reliable electricity, mission people and their Chinese friends gathered to pass the time with storytelling: accounts of horrifying tragedy, of narrow escapes, of mistresses or wayward sons, of ironic and unexpected outcomes, of love and devotion to family, and of soaring testimonials by Chinese Christians to their Christian faith.

In the verse collected in South Fukien: Missionary Poems, 1925-1951, William Angus records his unique views of the powerful way the Gospel influenced the lives of Chinese Christians and non-Christians alike. In a non-judgmental way, he relates their understandings and misunderstandings, frequently showing the distinctively Chinese spin on interpretations of lessons from the Bible. Always in counterpoint, though, is the force of China the country on the poet. Neither missionary nor Christian convert is ever far from the soil. Roads were traversed on foot. Crops flourished or failed at the caprice of the climate. Human excrement and animal manure were both essential to fertilize the cultivated fields. Predatory tigers and cynical, ruthless bandits lurked in the hills. Civil conflicts flared periodically between the Nationalists (Whites) and the Communists (Reds), with skirmishes into territory commanded by freelance warlords (Blacks). Men, women, and children were held for ransom. Unjust, arbitrary punishments were handed down, and people were shot or beheaded pointlessly.

Yet faith survived, and grew stronger. It flourishes in China today.

The linguistic background behind these poems deserves some comment. The Amoy (Xiamen) dialect, sometimes referred to as Min Na or Hokkien, dominates the southeastern quadrant of Fukien (Fujian) province, and a variant of the language is spoken on the island of Taiwan, settled by emigrants from the mainland. The dialect features seven tones, or intonations. That is, a particular syllable, such as "beh," may be pronounced in any of seven separate ways, each with its own meaning in context. The point here is that such variations require the speaker/listener to keep a sharp ear for subtleties of speech, for puns and jokes and twists of irony; storytelling becomes an exercise of great skill and art.

Educated city folk speak the formal, classic dialect with all its courtesies and graces, but the up-country Chinese in the towns and villages employ less refined variants that convey a broader, more earthy approach to daily expression.

William Angus loved the Amoy dialect and relished its nuances. He possessed a keen ear for the well-told story, complementing a sharp eye for the stark beauty of field, blossom, waterfall, or shining spirit. These elements can be seen throughout his verse, including his favorite poem, "The Three Trees," anthologized here. In many instances his poems are translations of oral narratives from the Chinese, innocent of decoration or artifice, yet deep enough to bless the reader with dual meanings for the price of one telling. These, and Angus's other narrative recollections, give insight into the Chinese mind, shaped by old, old wisdoms and traditional superstitions, stoically accepting of tragedy and death, and persevering through spare, optionless lives in the face of poverty and oppression. Ever pragmatic, however, the Chinese can embrace Christianity actively because of the storied quality of the Gospels, and because the Christian faith works, being based on love and compassion among a community of believers. It appeals as a faith whose history is well documented, and whose requirements are humane and remarkably simple in contrast to the strange and inordinate demands of ancestral spirits and idols for incense, special food, and fetishes.

Attempts to understand China are like plumbing an ocean. Even among its plainest people there is proud awareness of the great heft of China's culture, traditions, and history. What Westerners often mistake for xenophobia emerges as cultural exceptionalism: to the Chinese, theirs is a time-tested way of life, while the lifestyles of foreigners are outlandish and curious. Yet William Angus shows that the people are warmhearted, accepting, philosophical, and energetic in defending their Christian faith. Passions surge beneath the placid faces and deliberate movements of the people. They share with their missionary friends fondness for clever wordplay, a rollicking sense of humor, a love of gadgetry, and a zest for festive food and fragrant tea. Though the Chinese are also consummate actors and role-players, in dangerous real-life situations they often displayed intense loyalty to missionaries, even at the risk of their safety and lives.

So the Westerner who lives in China becomes aware gradually of this bond, this relationship that develops between himself and the host nation and people. William Angus was probably happier among the Chinese than he was "at home," in the States. Perhaps one does not "fall in love" with a country or become infatuated with it, but China demands respect, and it wins over the visitor with various blandishments, not the least of which are the power of its natural scenery and the varied, complex character of its people.

Spirituality is engrafted to the Chinese life from birth. Not a small part of its rhythms is superstition, embracing the season and moon phase at a child's natal day, portents signaled by the activities of animals, plots by evil spirits, and so forth. A common belief was that such spirits can travel only in a straight line; hence, a "spirit wall" was often erected before the main entrance to a dwelling, to ward off malevolent ghosts. (Indeed, ghost stories comprise an important genre in Chinese literature and folklore.)

On intellectual and intuitive levels, Chinese spiritual life is intertwined with physical and symbolic aspects of nature and their promptings to ethical behavior in humankind. Such thoughts evince deep intuitive relationships to social and human psychology. The South Fukien poems are replete with these kinds of intimations, especially in a rural context.

> Man models himself on earth,
> Earth on heaven,
> Heaven on the way,
> And the way on that which is naturally so.
>
> Tao Te Ching, XXV:58
> Trans. D. C. Lau
> (Penguin, 1963)

William Robertson Angus, Jr., was born in Manhattan on October 4, 1901, to William, Senior, and Agnes "Sue" Kenney Angus. He had one older brother, Robert Hevenor Angus. Their father was a retail grocer in the city who relocated his family in Oradell, Bergen County, New Jersey. William's mother died when he was a young boy. Two unmarried aunts assumed the maternal role, sharing the apartment above the grocery store in Oradell. William was an apt scholar, commuting to high school on the train, and playing football. His academic achievements earned him a scholarship from the State of New Jersey to attend Rutgers University, in New Brunswick. He enrolled in 1918, took the mandatory on-campus military training, and majored in soil fertility. He studied under the celebrated Selman Waksman, discoverer of the antibiotic streptomycin.

When the youthful William developed his Christian faith is not clear. His father was a Covenanter, a plain, conservative Scottish Presbyterian. His aunts, Lizzie and Mary Kenney, were no-nonsense spinsters, tough in more than their faith. It is possible that William was influenced in his decision to become a missionary by attending evangelistic summer camps on the shores of Lake George, in upstate New York. Upon his graduation from Rutgers, Phi Beta Kappa, in 1922, he approached various mission boards hoping to be commissioned as an agricultural missionary. In this hope, however, he was disappointed. The Dutch Reformed Church, now known as the Reformed Church in America, agreed to send him out into the field if he would first earn a Divinity degree. Accordingly, he attended Hartford Seminary in Connecticut, sometimes serving as a circuit rider on horseback in rural parts of Canada during the summers, and graduating in 1925 with a Bachelor of Sacred Theology degree.

In that year William presented himself again before the Board of Foreign Missions, RCA, in New York City, when he met for the first time the lovely young Agnes Buikema of Grand Rapids, Michigan, a recent graduate of Hope College, and a student at the Moody Bible Institute in Chicago. A subsequent Board decision sent them both to the Amoy Mission in South Fukien, China, where they were assigned the same teacher to study the local dialect. Their attraction for each other proved irresistible, and they became engaged. Agnes (or Joyce, as she later chose to call herself) had been assigned to the town of Sio-khe (Shange), and William was newly appointed to a post in Changchow (Zhangzhou), but they managed to see each other on weekends. William would walk the thirty miles upriver to Sio-khe on Saturday, and walk back to his duties in Changchow on Sunday. They married on Kulangsu Island (Gulangyu), July 5, 1927, to the discomfiture of the mission's elder single women, who felt that Agnes had forsaken her sacred obligations as a missionary as soon as the handsome, eligible preacher William had paid court.

They established a home in Changchow, where the mission owned Talmage College, a secondary school for young men, with residences for the American staff, and another compound with two large, square brick houses. The word "compound" suggests one of the paradoxes of the missionary lifestyle: generally they lived on property enclosed by a six-foot-high wall, separated from the noisy streets and the Chinese population, the same people to whom they offered the news of the Gospel, educational opportunities, and medical care and training. Such exclusivity seems antagonistic to the American attitudes of openness in society and belief in the virtue of diversity. Two points must be made, however: that the missionaries, despite their training and remarkable confidence, were easy prey for thieves and bandits without this kind of security; and that the living arrangements for Westerners in China usually shadowed the post-Edwardian British imperial style, with household servants (cook, waitpersons, a laundress, a handyman-gardener-messenger, and often a nursemaid or amah to mind the children), elevenses in the morning, tea in the afternoon, and fruit juice in the evening before bedtime—these, in addition to substantial breakfasts, lunches, and dinners. Those missionaries who chose also routinely used silver cutlery, fine china, and embroidered linens. For those missionaries assigned to remote stations lacking electricity, however, such amenities were not available, and the lifestyle was notably spartan.

Excused from commonplace tasks, mission workers were free to undertake humanitarian activities—teaching classes, planning sermons, operating on patients, conducting meetings, reading extensively, and writing reams of correspondence. Angus, like other evangelical missionaries, traveled regularly afield in the districts surrounding the cities to which he was assigned, and his encounters with the people were fully as extensive as his more than 600 China poems give witness. A virtual circuit rider again, he monitored pastorless churches, shared joy with Chinese converts in services and gatherings, and supervised mission business in remote villages—down to negotiating with regional bandits. Angus and his colleagues customarily received their instructions at the essential yearly mission meeting which took place at the field headquarters on Kulangsu, where budgets were reviewed, personnel assignments were made, and policy was formulated. Often a field secretary sent from the board of foreign missions in New York was present at these gatherings. It was also a time for mission parties, especially around July Fourth.

Mission housing was usually of native brick, or brick-and-stucco, with wide verandahs for cooling breeze and shade. Windows could be shuttered in typhoon weather. Wood-burning fireplaces graced the major rooms, to be used in chilly mountain or winter temperatures.

In several instances mission compounds featured tennis courts, to encourage personal fitness. Always there was danger of disease, however. Mission families regularly received inoculations for cholera, plague, smallpox, tetanus, typhoid, and the usual "children's diseases." There was ever the risk of contracting anthrax, dengue, dysentery, malaria, or parasitic worms, or of being poisoned by spoiled food bought and eaten in the streets. Several families in the Amoy mission lost young children due to disease or accidental death.

The mission children were customarily home schooled, in small groups where several families resided nearby. Beginning at the ninth grade, Western students were, in normal times, sent off to the Shanghai American School as boarders. Families returned to the States on furlough every seventh year for personal renewal, and importantly, to reaffirm contacts with sponsoring churches by sermons and testimonials about work in the field. These were circumstances that came into play as the Anguses negotiated vocational and personal lives between two nations.

The family had just returned from furlough in 1931, a stay divided between Princeton, New Jersey, and Grand Rapids, when Communist fighters occupied Changchow. William and Joyce Angus and their new baby, Margery, had to flee the city in April 1932. Their mission house became the headquarters of Mao Tse-tung (Mao Zedong), and most of their possessions were stolen or destroyed. Thereafter, they fulfilled various assignments until 1938, when they returned to the States again, this time with two additional children, sons David and John. That year the mission board gave early furloughs in concern over the Japanese incursions in the north.

Chinese New Year, 1940, saw the Anguses returned to the Amoy mission, where William immersed himself in the travels on mission business that occupied so much of his attention. The family was assigned briefly to Sio-khe, but brought back to the then still-free Kulangsu station when hostilities with the Japanese seemed imminent. Attentive as always to the needs of the Chinese church, William crossed the Japanese and Chinese lines in September 1941 for a series of meetings around the mission territory. When the attack on Pearl Harbor occurred in December, he found himself prevented from entering an occupied Kulangsu from "Free China," while his family became civilian prisoners of war in the international settlement. Later, Joyce and the three children were evacuated to Shanghai in April 1942, as part of a Red Cross-sponsored prisoner exchange and repatriation. From Shanghai they sailed on June 30 for Singapore, Mozambique, Brazil, and New York City, arriving in America on August 25. It goes without saying that almost all of the Anguses' household goods and personal possessions, left hurriedly behind, once more were either looted or destroyed.

Joyce Angus and the children made their home in Grand Rapids during the war years, and were not reunited with William until March 1946, in the United States. The mission board next sent the Anguses to New Haven, Connecticut, to study Mandarin Chinese at the Yale language school. The next spring Rutgers University awarded William an honorary Doctorate in Divinity. In September 1947, William, Joyce, and the boys returned to China. Margery remained in the States as a Hope College student. The parents and son John joined other colleagues in Leng-na (Longyan), about 120 miles distant from the coastline, while David attended the Shanghai American School.

Soon, though, the Red Army pressed its winning campaign from the north on Fukien Province. David and other mission students were evacuated from Shanghai in April 1949, returning to South Fukien. Over the ensuing summer, David and John made plans to continue their education at the Brent School in Baguio, the Philippines. About a year later the Communists swept into Leng-na as the Nationalists withdrew toward Taiwan. Because Leng-na had been occupied by the Reds in the 'thirties, it was deemed technically "liberated," and supposedly the new liberators were to be more lenient than their armies had been with towns long sympathetic to the Chiang Kai-shek (Jiang Jieshi) regime. Interrogations and mass executions of the local citizens soon showed that such leniency was highly imaginary. With their children offshore, William and Joyce remained, under increasingly ticklish circumstances eventually leading to the near-compulsory exit of all Christian missionaries. Permission for them to leave Leng-na was not granted until Easter, 1951. For a third time the Anguses were forced to relinquish most of their worldly goods.

After enjoying a furlough in the States the following year, William and Joyce were re-assigned to the Philippines, primarily to work with communities of overseas Chinese in that country. After serving three terms—in Cagayan de Oro, Legaspi, and Quezon City—William and Joyce Angus retired, forty-year veterans of service in the mission field. They eventually settled in Orange City, Iowa, where William purchased his first house. There, Joyce died in 1973. William continued to revise the large corpus of writings he called China Poems, from which this selection is taken, and to complete the immense task, begun in the Philippines, of paraphrasing the entire Bible into verse. This work he continued until his death in Orange City in 1984.

In South Fukien: Missionary Poems 1925-1951, William Angus leaves an important legacy. That the poems reveal a highly personal and appreciative view of his encounters with the Chinese and their culture is indisputable. Moreover, his writings comprise a vital historic document, related with a storyteller's gift in cadences as engaging as those of common speech.

The surviving members of the Angus family gratefully acknowledge the dedicated work of the editor of South Fukien, scholar and archivist David Andrews, who has read carefully and collated the often revised versions of William Angus's typescripts. Mr. Andrews has selected sixty of the most representative and expressive poems from among the five volumes the missionary had written over the years. This selection speaks well for the gifts of the poet, and for the spirit of the Chinese people. The family is also indebted to Dr. Paul Vander Meer, Professor Emeritus, Geography Department, California State University at Fresno, for his enthusiastic encouragement and willingness to review this work in its developing stages.

David Robertson Angus
Lansing, Michigan, April 2014

INTRODUCTION

It perhaps goes without saying that danger is a vocational commonplace for the missionary. The news headlines—lately from North Korea, Mexico, and Peru—yearly remind us. Missionaries are routinely stationed in countries undergoing political disorder that has long preceded their arrival (sometimes their births) and often outlasts their tenure.

Such sojourners for faith are among the most watched persons in foreign communities—liable by word or deed, or by their mere presence, to incur suspicion, contradiction, misinterpretation, rejection, worse. Trust can be earned; tolerance, even survival, is won by circumspect behavior. And to act with circumspection implies a reciprocal close evaluation of persons encountered and situations emerging.

William Angus would have learned this serving as a missionary in China during its twentieth-century struggle for national identity. From his first years there Angus faced unbelievers, outright opponents, and converts caught between tradition and Christian faith. He later dealt with Kuomintang government officials, marauding bandits, Nationalist and Communist soldiers, Japanese occupiers, and finally People's Republic ideologues.

Village and city life in China held the social mandate that one's public image was subject to scrutiny that could bring disapproval. The lives of Christian converts and unbelievers alike were concerned with maintaining dignity against rebuke that would shame one's family, make one an object of derision or complaint, or make one seem subject to foreign influence.[1] This cultism of reputation took on larger, fatal dimensions under revolution and war. On taking power the Communists were able to use this native proclivity to establish societal control.

1. The Chinese senses of dignity and shame, and their relation to period missionary work, are illuminated in a 1929 essay by Joseph Rutten, a Belgian Catholic priest. "Les obstacles à l'évangélisation de la Chine," in *Museum Lessianum*, Section Missiologique, "Obstacles à l'apostalat" (Louvain: Editions du Museum Lessianum); excerpts in translation appear as "Christian Conversion in China, Source of Shame or Pride?" in Jessie G. Lutz, ed., *Christian Missions in China* (1965).

In working with the Chinese, Angus witnessed, or heard told of, the fortunes of a young man forbidden to worship Christ because neighbors would call him an unworthy son; of a young woman who drowned herself because others doubted that a world war was the only impediment to her fiancé's return; of a merchant who feared gossip that he denied children shelter during a bombing raid; of a village afraid of reprisals for being forced to hide a bandit leader's supplies; of a righteous school superintendent imprisoned as "unpatriotic" by the Communists.[2] These were not the only fortunes in Chinese lives during Angus's quarter-century in-country. He witnessed joys as well, and errors in men and women's judgment, endurance under poverty and political confusion, and sincere accession to faith.

It was all recorded in what one contemporary referred to as Angus's "journals." The mistake was an honest one, given the reportorial quality of the writings the missionary gave him to read. For Angus applied his accustomed circumspection to a life's work of narrative poetry not only aesthetically fine, but an important documentation of rural life in twentieth-century China, and of the experience of a small provincial area at the border of a great clamor for national definition.

Henry James urged the writer to be the sort of person on whom nothing is lost. Bill Angus became that sort among the Chinese people and amid their changing times. His missionary service also brought him to discover the depths of his vocation, embrace them, and through his verse share them with our times.

Amoy and Points West

In September 1925 the newly ordained Reverend William Angus arrived at Amoy City (now Xiamen) on the island of Amoy, located in the Formosa Strait just off the Chinese mainland province of Fukien (Fujian). In the autumn heat, he wore the same wool suit in which he had shipped out from chilly Vancouver, British Columbia. A tall man with a tall man's shyness—a trait remarked upon to the end of

2. These situations are featured in the poems "Lotus," "The Arm," "The Tiger's Things," and "Tribute to the Sims," respectively.

his days—Angus was unsure of his mission as an ordained minister. On graduating college three years earlier, he had petitioned to be sent to China as an agricultural missionary—an expert on row crops and seeding yields. The Board of Foreign Missions of the Reformed Church, an American, Calvinist-based denomination, would not seek to fill that position for another twenty-seven years—in part, perhaps, to avoid any instance of the perennial charges that Western missionaries were meddlers in Chinese cultural affairs.[3] When, in rebuilding its humanitarian programs after World War II, the Board granted the Amoy Mission's request for an agriculturalist, the Mission was but a year away from the harassment by the new communist government that led Angus and other Reformed missionaries to exit the country, despite assurances by the convert faithful that current political circumstances, like the others their church had known, would soon enough pass.

Wanting to see, and serve, China, Angus took a Divinity degree, and through to 1951 served there as an evangelist, teacher, and administrator. His pastoral longings (in the other sense of the adjective), found expression in cultivating the life of South Fukien in narrative verse, a selection of which makes up this volume. The preface by his son, David, well records Angus's missionary career. This introduction sets that career in the context of China missions history, and of the critical years of prolonged revolution, world war and its economic aftermath, and drastic political revision that Angus's verse defines as epochs of twentieth-century China. These were, as the famed native imprecation has it, "interesting times." Angus's gifts, however, convert that curse into a grace upon our times, revealed now just over a half-century after the

3. Funding concerns may have been a factor, and as well thoughts of a shortage of missionary recruits in the previous decade. Yet, as it had been since Christian missionaries arrived in China, to be perceived as interfering in relations between convert tenant farmers and large landholders was potentially hazardous for missionaries and converts both. In 1922 a joint effort of the National Conference of Churches (U.S.) and the Christian-founded University of Nanking initiated an agricultural improvement program that aided some areas of Fukien without involving missionaries.

poet unwillingly left his pastures. Through Angus's verse we encounter these China years anew.

Among Reformed mission territories, Angus was assigned to what was then one of China's more pacific provinces, emissary of a Church that established there hospitals, practical and theological schools, and a splay of churches and outstation chapels on Amoy Island and across a mainland area extending only some 50 miles north of, and 120 miles to the northwest and southwest of, Amoy City. But even rural Fukien would become a dangerous place for missionary work. The southerly corner ministered to by the Reformed Church, in cooperation with two English Protestant missionary societies, would be under both distant and close threat of harm to missionaries and converts, despite the Church's dedication to fostering an ecumenical Chinese Protestant church entirely administrated and supported by natives.[4]

While Roman Catholic missions had been founded in China by the end of the sixteenth century, Protestant missionaries arrived only early in the nineteenth century, and the wide establishment of their missions began only after 1858. Protestant missions owed their existence to the adventurous benevolence of supporting churches and supervising mission boards oceans away. But mission furtherance depended on trade and diplomacy, most specifically the "gunboat diplomacy" that protected Western trade inroads, early and late. This military extortion of Western rights within a China controlled by the last dynasts of the Manchu empire began in the first British opium war ending in 1842,

4. The predominantly Congregationalist London Missionary Society and the mission of the Presbyterian Church in England had churches and outstation chapels in the geographical bounds of the Reformed Church's Amoy Mission, and others beyond it. After some seventy years' cooperation, the three missions formed the South Fukien United Church in 1920. In 1927 the Synod joined the ecumenical Church of Christ in China, a larger movement toward an "indigenous" church that advanced the longtime goals of the several Protestant missions in China to create a self-supporting church of native ecclesiastics and lay administrators. Angus's verse testifies to the extent to which mission-created churches exercised native autonomy.

in which naval force overcame Chinese resistance to the importation of India opium as a trade good.[5] Peacemaking brought about the hated "unequal treaties" favoring British imports over Chinese exports. Afterward France, Belgium, Germany, Russia, Japan, and the United States sued for competitive trade treaties, which the Manchus granted to stave off invasion. Over time the treaties secured foreign access to ocean and river seaports (including Amoy), then the creation of foreign and international settlements untouchable by Chinese law, and grants of foreign-controlled industrial districts. Giving extraterritorial concessions led to accepting extravagant loans from the trading powers, which China needed to maintain its dynastic government, adopt industry and railroads to compete in modern trade, and buy war materiel to keep the worst threats of foreign exploitation at bay.

By the end of the century the most feared threat was from a rapidly modernizing Japan that coveted China's land and resources. Non-Asian nations and their representatives in China, however, bore the brunt of public disfavor. Like Japan and Russia, the Western nations were labeled "imperialists"—encroaching foreign powers striving to subjugate and exploit less developed nations. But because their churches sent Christian missionaries the Western nations stood accused of a greater subversiveness: the wish to make China over in the Western cultural image. Missionaries became suspected agents of Western hegemony, in all its dimensions. They were so long vilified as such that in the twenty years after they were compelled to leave China their writings and the studies written about them pondered the extent to which they were consciously or unconsciously so.

Under the first trade treaties, Protestant missionaries followed the

5. Sovereignty issues were of as much concern as the narcotic. The Chinese had imported opium from southwest Asia and grown it internally (in Fukien and other provinces) since the first century, CE. Demand increased upon a late-seventeenth-century population explosion. When India-based British merchants sought money equity for their Chinese tea exports, the insular Chinese refused any British good but opium. Reciprocity for lost trade in other products was achieved by flooding of China with the drug, incurring much resentment.

sailors and diplomats of their countries to China, often traveling for convenience on military or merchant ships—a development that helped initiate distrust. The founding Reformed Church missionaries took this opportunity, first arriving at Canton (Guangzhou) on an American merchantman in 1842. Resentment at the perceived missionary intent to displace China's ancient spiritual and cultural values by the mandarin Confucian scholars in provincial office spread to a majority of the public, keeping missionaries of the time bottled up in the treaty ports. Evangelists that dared to strike out upon the mainland were met with hostility or indifference. But the Reformed cohort found the poor and least of Amoy Island and the neighboring island of Kulangsu (Gulangyu) friendly, and receptive churchgoers.[6] To communicate and preach, the Amoy missionaries painstakingly overcome language and dialect difficulties. Their hearers spread not only their words to the mainland, but also religious tracts printed in Chinese characters. Though conversions would be years in the making, soon the curious and the spiritually inclined of such later centers of missionary activity as Changchow (Zhangzhou), Tong-an (Tongan), and Chioh-be (Shima), and of even farther regions, were attending services on the islands. A Romanized version of the Amoy dialect was next developed to teach the illiterate to read Scripture in translation. Missionary wives surmounted the bars of gender and modesty to introduce Fukienese women to the Gospels.

The treaty ending the second opium war mandated Chinese state tolerance of Christianity, and the other Western nations followed Britain in demanding missionary rights. Converts could now be sought inland as well at the ports, though to the end their number was small within

6. The first Reformed missionaries at Amoy operated under the offices of the ecumenical American Board of Commissioners for Foreign Missions, which sent missionaries of other denominations as well. Missionaries of the American Presbyterian church and the two British missionary organizations cited were also operating at Amoy before 1850 was out. The Reformed Church's own Board of Foreign Missions assumed direction of the Church's missionaries in 1857.

great China—estimated at less than one percent of the population.[7] Popular and official displeasure with missionaries continued through the waning years of the dynasty, and missionaries made easy targets for animadversion. They were unarmed and frequently alone, or provokingly surrounded by solicitous converts. Their purposes were obscure to the vast uninitiated, and their practices tended to separate convert from community: they established schools, forbade ancestor worship, and disparaged foot-binding and the subjugation of women. Their presence and travel privileges were secured by foreign might—well into the twentieth century missionaries embodied the shame of the "unequal treaties." Acting with seeming impunity, they bought or rented property where they were not desired. Some were known to interfere in legal action brought against converts (often unpopular large landholders or merchants) and to shield them from arrest. Folk ignorance, often fomented by political agents, could accuse missionaries of any number of crimes, from secret atrocities and sacrilege to profiteering. And at the capital, Peking (Beijing), there was always suspicion that a Christianizing China would imbibe Western democracy, promising discord to a country that was less a governed nation than a culturally bound set of disparate provinces.

The Amoy Mission was territorially limited and always greatly understaffed. While it was far from inland Peking, and removed from the volatile, foreigner-crowded cities of Canton, Shanghai, and Nanking (Nanjing), resentment primed on more visible and far-ranging Westerners colored attitudes toward rural missionaries. The Western-style housing and amenities enjoyed by most Protestant missionaries, which David Angus recalls in his preface, came under particular objection through several eras of nineteenth- and twentieth-century reaction. This lifestyle gave missionaries and their families protection and comforting ties to Western traditions. But to irate dynastic or nationalist Chinese the practice implied a basic, and hypocritical, aloofness by missionaries toward their host people. In

7. Cited by Jessie G. Lutz in the introduction to *Christian Missions in China*, vii.

turn, access to missionary compounds was said to entice Chinese into spurning their roots for Western ways to achieve a higher standard of living. The foreign-paid missionaries were also thought to be living at an unseemly higher standard than the Chinese they moved among. (In the case of the Amoy Mission, this prejudice tarred the ordained native pastors paid by their congregations, and the convert preachers even less well paid by the Reformed Church missions board.) Thus missionaries, already viewed as teachers of a Christian submissiveness that would make Chinese susceptible to exploitation by Western capitalists, were further reviled as being akin to factory and shipping overlords in their purchasing power. Perceptions of economic disparity affected William Angus and his family several times.[8]

Perceptions can make history, but in this case not facts. Missionaries were distinctly less well off than Western capitalists based in China, and never profited through exploiting native labor, manual or ecclesiastical. Amoy Mission pastors' salaries were low because congregations could not manage to pay them more: the native-controlled Church envisioned by the missions board would be increasingly called upon to support itself. Contributions from American Reformed churches that might have might have been used to raise preachers' salaries were needed to sustain schools, hospitals, churches, and chapels. Moreover, as both missions and Western-owned industry grew in the decades preceding the First World War, many China-stationed capitalists

8. Amoy Mission converts of the mid-1920s expressed to Angus their displeasure with missionary salaries. In 1927, during the Nationalist activity supporting the Northern Expedition, Angus's school students at the city of Sio-khe became outspoken in their newly fashionable condemnation of the missionary lifestyle. In 1932, troops of the Chinese Communist Party occupied the mission compound at Changchow, where the Anguses were stationed, and dispersed the family's possessions among the populace (relived in the poem "After the Looting"). Under the People's Republic of China, mission compounds were subjected to random visits by awestruck peasant soldiers of the revolution, indoctrinated with the idea that all property belonged to the state. When officials compelled missionaries at Leng-na (Longyan) to move to new quarters the Anguses' possessions were again looted.

resented missionaries for complicating the Chinese laborer's mind with notions of egalitarianism and justice derived from the Gospels, even as their pious brethren at home pumped philanthropic funds into the missionary enterprise.

For supposed creatures of a rapacious foreign power, American missionaries were rather poorly protected. Their regional consulates gave them warnings and afforded shelter from danger when possible, but were effectively powerless to stop anti-missionary uprisings, about which they could merely protest later, demanding that Chinese troops protect beleaguered missionaries. Concern in Washington for American missionaries varied over time and circumstance, ranging from expressions of earnest regard bestowed on mission board heads to private espousals that the missionary in China was a nuisance, and forever a liability to diplomatic and trade relations.

Regional uprisings against missionaries were frequent in the nineteenth century. In Foochow (Fuzhou), Fukien's provincial capital, two British missions' buildings were destroyed in 1864. Facilities belonging to the English societies collaborating in the Amoy Mission met the same end in Chuanchow (Quanzhou), 1866, and Foochow again, 1878. At Chienning (Jianning), beginning in 1863, mob actions kept Anglican missions from taking root for twenty years, and disturbed them again in 1892. In 1899 an attack by the vanguard of the Boxer Rebellion finally put them to the torch, with one convert murdered and three missionaries barely escaping the mob.[9] Anger against neighboring Catholic missionaries over the Franco-Chinese War led to destruction of Catholic and Protestant properties alike in Fukien and other provinces. (As late as 1906 an animus against Catholics rose in South Fukien, this time at Changpu [Zhangbu].) The most notorious local outrage took place at the village of Huashan in 1895. There, a secret

9. By their example, the "Boxers," or Society of Righteous and Harmonious Fists, inspired other Chinese to violent actions against foreigners both before and during their short but widespread terror campaign. President McKinley's dangerously presumptive 1899 Open Door proposal, asking foreign nations to share Chinese concessions equally, fired their anti-Americanism.

society tormented a convert it held a grudge against; his complaints brought government soldiers, and in the next month retaliation against area missionaries. In an armed attack, eleven British missionaries were killed and an American Methodist woman injured.[10]

The 1900 Boxer revolt against state tolerance of foreign exploitation brought murder and atrocity on hundreds of converts and missionaries far to the northeast, putting Fukien missionaries on fearful alert. A pitiless, unsparing Western military invasion followed, its vengeful American force led by an American missionary. Missionary colleagues joined American imperialists in supporting the treaty right of military intervention, however vehement. The press coverage invited a backlash, in which America's social critics (Mark Twain among them) questioned the motives of the missionary enterprise and its reliance on guns and armies. Some liberal discontent can be traced to missionary attitudes exhibited over the previous sixty years.[11] Early missionaries had chafed at their confinement to the treaty ports and their rejection by the mandarin bureaucratic culture. A number advocated military opening of the Chinese interior to missionaries. Sentiments were registered to the effect that cannon balls might be better dispersed than Christian piety. Once religious tolerance was obtained by threat and treaty, calls to send a Western fleet were heard whenever missionaries were confronted by the danger their pursuits attracted. Missionary writings, read avidly at home, adopted military metaphors for the evangelistic effort: missionaries were "conquering" heathen China for the Savior. Resistance was the work of "the Enemy," a satanic designation that could easily lose its distinguishing capital letter. Tendentious and derogatory characterizations of the Chinese proliferated, as if they were barbarians destined to be urged toward Christianity by the flat

10. Kenneth S. Latourette, *A History of Christian Missions in China* (1929), 468-471, 501, 616; Paul A. Varg, *Missionaries, Chinese, and Diplomats* (1958), 39-40.

11. American Progressives were also disturbed by reports of the denaturing effect the missionary presence had wrought upon the natives of Tahiti and the Hawaiian Islands, and by the bloody denial of democracy to the conquered Philippines.

of Charlemagne's fallen sword, wielded again by the West. Missionary frustration expressed itself further in writings displaying contempt for Chinese culture and customs.[12]

Reforms of mission values followed the Boxer Rebellion and the American imperialist era of overseas expedition. Protestant ministers at home and abroad turned to a "social gospel" approach in line with the Progressive movement in politics. Overt evangelism was subordinated to programs bringing humanitarian aid to the downtrodden. In overseas missions, new organizational attention was given to the building and maintaining of hospitals and schools, and the education of doctors, nurses, and teachers. Protestantism itself underwent a theological shift to a liberal modernism that recognized the universal spirituality of man across religious and cultural boundaries. In missions, the "New Theology" sought to teach Christianity and encourage conversion as expressions of the human desire to know the Creator. Under these revised conceptions of the Christian mission, missionaries reevaluated their dependence on home governments and resisted calling for military aid when changing political fortunes in China offered threats to their lives. They now found in humility and service the Christ-like qualities once sought in militancy. The shift in attitude was so effectual that older converts at the Amoy Mission of the 1920s complained that missionaries, in their politic dispassion, no longer acted like fathers toward them.

This was the climate that William Angus encountered in 1925. Redeeming breezes tempered the residual heat of nearly a century of common misunderstanding. But other, superheated forces were massing to issue winds of change.

The Mission

By 1925 the Amoy Mission had become a familiar and respected institution in the life of South Fukien. Its purview now reached nearly its farthest extent, to almost eighty widespread outstations—a few

12. These were prevalent attitudes, but not universal ones. The extent to which Reformed missionaries in China embraced them awaits further study.

supported their own churches, the rest had subsidized chapels and meeting places. Evangelism and human aid were directed from four district centers: Amoy City, Changchow to the west, Sio-khe (Shange) to the southwest near present-day Pinghe, and Leng-na (Longyan) in the mountainous North River upcountry. While the number of serving Reformed missionaries was at an all-time high—forty-six[13]—they ministered among an estimated four million Chinese, distributed through the hundreds of villages surrounding each of the district centers. Like other China missions, Amoy made full use of missionary wives as teachers and evangelists among women, and the Reformed Church was at the forefront of American churches that early on trained single women for missionary work in education, nursing, and school and hospital administration.

In the cities, evangelism was alive in street preaching, Sunday schools, and reading rooms that doubled as youth centers. It was spread beyond the cities by missionary visits to outstation churches and chapels, particularly those chapels not served by a native preacher. In the best of times, however, those missionaries available for district circuit travel could visit each village at most twice yearly. They reached the far-flung stations by a combination of means: steam launches or motor boats, mules or horses, hired sedan chairs, and—always and eventually—by foot through mountains and valleys as beautiful as their broken paths were tiring. Less frequently a rail connection was available, or (depending on the existence of roads) a lift in an automobile or a seat in an omnibus converted from a freight truck. Though Angus wrote many of his poems on furlough from China, between six-year missionary terms, we might imagine him turning over in his mind the narrative sources and personal experiences that shaped his work during his overland journeys from station to station.

The journeymen evangelists slept rough on chapel benches, in the varying comforts of the "prophet's room" kept for them at churches, or at rude country inns along the route. At an outstation the missionary

13. Their ranks, and those of the native clergy, would thin in the coming decades and be disrupted by World War II.

would hold services, visit converts' homes, assist in any administrative necessities, and often take part in "Gospel Band" expeditions—evangelistic forays in which local pastors and preachers would proceed from a host church into the neighboring villages to preach and sing. Following the plan for fostering a native church, evangelism was kept vital in the absence of missionaries by the continuing work of pastors and preachers, enthused lay people, and the "Bible women" who preached among their sex.

By the time of Angus's early work as a teacher at Sio-khe, the Mission operated schools at the elementary through post-secondary levels and sent its students on to union-effort Christian colleges, universities, and theological schools. Though mission-based education was still suspect in a China struggling toward nationalism, some Chinese saw it as an opportunity for their children that their own government neglected. Mission efforts made it possible for many Chinese to become educated, prepare for college or university, study nursing or medicine, become preachers or teachers, and in many cases, become officials or leaders. Bleak village life—especially so for girls and single women—could be redeemed by a new spirit of community.

Mission-run hospitals earned widespread favor. The Amoy Mission administrated five hospitals at Kulangsu, Sio-khe, Tong-an, and Leng-na in the distant north, dispensing health services as far-ranging as dentistry, opthalmic care, and opium addiction cures. Half or more of the hospital work was performed as charity. The majority of hospital staff was made up of mission-educated natives, who offered a gentle, non-programmatic evangelism to patients already impressed with the civility and effectiveness of their care.

As with all evangelistic efforts, though, the converts made were of quality but not of quantity. Reformed missionaries in China now managed an exponentially greater number of patients and students than converts; the twentieth century saw a peak number of just under 4,000 communicants in 1938, the year the Japanese occupied Fukien's offshore islands.[14] It was roughly .1 percent of the Mission territory's

14. Quoted from the church's Board of Foreign Missions annual report in

population, though the number of churchgoers did not approach the number of lives that Reformed missionaries and their converts touched and improved. Conversions were hampered by the customs of ancestor and idol worship, the enmeshing clan system of extended family relationships, and the pressure exerted on the individualistic impulse by community opinion—as Angus demonstrates in the poem "Holdout."[15] But others sought in the Mission pipeline an increase in personal freedom.

The Dynasts

The good work of the Amoy Mission accelerated even as the political situation altered. In 1911 the decrepit Manchu dynasty yielded to a nationalist revolution, the expression of a widespread urge to create amid China's internal divisions a republican solidarity against perceived and real foreign encroachments. The transition was long incomplete, and uncertain of leadership. Sun Yat-sen, regarded as the father of republicanism, had little military backing. Powerful rivals for executive office had more, and with his ideological opponents put Sun in and out of power until 1923, and thereafter threatened his rule until his premature death in 1925—the year William Angus arrived at Amoy City. Yet Sun's Nationalist political party, the Kuomintang (Guomindang), prevailed over a resurgence of empire, the menace of warring regional military governments, and internecine rivalries. Missionaries supported Kuomintang nationalism, with its ideals of constitutionalism and parliamentary government, as progress toward democratic reforms that would improve lives and allow individual religious freedom. In 1923, the year Sun, declared premier of the Republic of China, sought foreign aid to unify China by force, a diverse group of American missionaries requested that no military action be taken by their country in the event

Gerald F. De Jong, *The Reformed Church in China 1842–1951* (1992), 205. De Jong's book provides a commendable account of Amoy Mission activities through two centuries.

15. In Père Joseph Rutten's observation, China's religious distinctions had devolved to individual cults of folk religion without doctrine, but with a common feature of ancestor worship. Lutz, ed., 28.

they would be endangered or harmed in the Kuomintang attempt to establish its government.

Sun, and his successor Chiang Kai-shek (Jiang Jieshi), faced the opposition invited by the political ties that they and their rivals made. Radical thought in China had found affinities with Russian communism. The Kuomintang had to recognize a left wing in the Chinese Communist Party (CCP) formed in 1921, and draw on its strength to militarily unify China. In the near-chaos of the early republic Sun's rivals for executive power either were, or were supported by, competing *tuchüns*, or regional warlords, whose armies continually fought those not commanded by temporary allies. In the absence of a strong central government with a hierarchy down to the village level, the warlords and their vassals seized various regions and even entire provinces, killing their opposition and financing their operations by imposing hard taxes and opium farming on the peasants. Tiu^{n} [16] Ge, a bandit commander subordinate to a more powerful *tuchün*, controlled a sizable part of the Amoy Mission territory, growing opium until ousted by Kuomintang troops in 1926. Next— as some of Angus's most compelling verse records—South Fukien, like other areas relieved of warlord control, was menaced by unaffiliated bandit armies and gangs, adding to regional disorder.[17] A few of these bandit commanders that Chiang could not destroy once he established his government he made Nationalist army commanders, putting each at the head of 10,000 men (including their former banditti) for as long as

16. In all of his typescripts, Angus used the superscript *n* to represent a nasal *n* sound that is imposed on some word endings in proper names and place names in the Amoy dialect. This sound is sometimes used at the end of the first word of a two-word name to elide the syllables together in pronunciation.

17. Minor banditry was a fluid career path. Varieties of men rode under outlaws great and small, pegging their fortunes to the shifting loyalties of their commanders. Some commanders became wealthy, territorial masters, collaborating with the Nationalist or Communist sides; some were assassinated. Others led non-political "Black" armies of uniformed freebooters. The least ran gangs of roadside robbers. The reader of Angus's poems should always look for cues to the sophistication and affiliation of his bandits.

their fealty held. To secure regional control, Chiang made high generals out of *tuchüns* willing to bargain with him, and deployed them to battle other warlords allied against him in the north and south, some of which craved governing in his place.

To maintain his Nationalist government, Chiang had to balance needed communist political and military support within the Kuomintang against the financial and military assistance given him by right-leaning *tuchüns,* large landholders, urban capitalists, and organized crime bosses. These hated the CCP and feared the Soviet Union, which aided and advised not only the Chinese Communists but also Chiang—and Sun before him. In 1926 Kuomintang armies under a Nationalist-Communist coalition embarked from their southern power bases on a three-pronged Northern Expedition to overrun opposing warlords and unify China by revolutionary force. The western-ranging arm of the Expedition marched through Fukien on its way to help seize Shanghai and Nanking. During 1926 William Angus would see South Fukien's cities papered with anti-Western propaganda posters put up by the Communist troops of the alliance, and witness revolutionary rallies that denounced imperialism and those unlucky citizens said to favor foreign interlopers—events movingly recorded in the poem "Not Ashamed." When the Expedition reached Nanking in March 1927, violence against foreign institutions ensued, with six Westerners killed. American Marines were dispatched, and the consulate called Reformed missionaries working upcountry, including Angus and his wife, down to the safety of the international settlement on Kulangsu.

Deferring to its communist wing and to anti-Western nationalists, the Kuomintang in 1926 required mission schools to register with the state and refrain from religious education. But other concessions to the Communists were to be curtailed and abandoned. Despite the prospects of fighting northern warlords to capture Peking, which occurred through 1928, and of an opportunistic invasion by Japan, which began in 1931, the Kuomintang broke with Moscow, expelled the Communists, and liquidated many thousands of CCP members and left-wing fellow travelers in cities under KMT control, including

Foochow.[18] The Communist armies headquartered in the rural south organized peasant rebellions; one of the longest-lasting efforts involved the seizure and holding of the Leng-na area of the Amoy Mission's northern territory, 1928–1932. Troops there redistributed the large landholders' acreage among the peasantry, but the next year marred their public service with contrarian acts of occupying and destroying the Mission hospital and imprisoning its medical missionary.

Betrayed by once-friendly warlords who now went over to Chiang, the Communist armies retreated into rural Soviets, remote strongholds scattered through south-central China. Before retiring to the Kiangsi (Jiangxi) Soviet, straddling the mountainous border of Kiangsi and Fukien provinces, forces commanded by Mao Tse-tung (Mao Zedong) occupied Changchow, turning out the Anguses when Mao took the missionary compound for his headquarters. Within two years the Nationalist government at the new capital, Nanking, put down an upstart rival government created in Fukien by a coalition of southern politicians and disaffected army commanders originally sent by Chiang to dislodge the Communists—a development that brought destructive air raids on Changchow. Consequences of the uprising are addressed in several of Angus's poems, as are those of the "Bandit Suppression Campaigns" that Chiang directed mainly against the Communists of the rural Soviets and scattered country outposts. The campaigns forced Mao to lead the Kiangsi Soviet armies on the famous 1934 "Long March" to safety in the far northwest.

Increasing threat of a full Japanese invasion lessened persecution of the Communists and created a nominally united military front, besmirched with internecine warring even after the Japanese overran

18. Japan despised China for its internal struggles and drift toward communism, and at the same time feared having its traders in inland China and military forces in Manchuria expelled by any single or coalition anti-imperialist government that might emerge from the fray. In 1931 it invaded northern provinces below Manchuria, then halted, under truce, humiliatingly close to Peking in 1933. The Japanese installed the "last emperor," the former boy ruler Pu-yi, as executive of the new puppet state of Manchukuo.

northeastern China in 1937—taking Nanking, brutally, and Shanghai. In the next year Japan invaded China's southeastern coastal regions and inlands. Japanese naval and infantry forces occupied Fukien's offshore islands in May 1938, but left the Amoy Mission's upcountry territory part of "Free China." As churches and other buildings on Amoy were shelled, then taken over by soldiers, refugees streamed to the mainland and onto Kulangsu, whose international status was not yet violated. The Mission fed thousands of fleeing Chinese, sheltered them in schools and hospitals, and participated in an international relief effort.

The Anguses, with their children, returned from a stateside furlough in 1939, taking up duties in Sio-khe until tensions between Japan and the U.S. called for missionaries with families to decamp for the international settlement. Still, through the end of 1941, Angus crossed over to the mainland to evangelize and assist the ten remaining upcountry missionaries in administrative duties accelerated by the need to work around the occupation. After the Pearl Harbor attack Kulangsu was taken, and Angus and another married missionary were cut off from their families, who were later repatriated. The poet's response to this emotional separation, which lasted more than four years, finds terse, understated expression in the poem "Why We Forgot."

The Mission hospital buildings on Kulangsu were made internment centers for Allied POWs. Wartime inflation drove up the cost of medicine, supplies and food, a trend that would increase into disastrous consequences in postwar China. Bombing and depredation by Japanese troops ruined hospitals and schools, while roads and bridges between the Mission outstations were destroyed to confound Japanese advances. Through the war, Angus served as the Amoy Mission's sole itinerant evangelist, making a circuit of 300 miles among the North River mountain villages alone, and traveling the two other district circuits as well. As the Pacific Theater situation worsened the remaining missionaries on Kulangsu were allowed to repatriate along with hundreds of non-Reformed missionaries from other occupied zones. Out of concern for their safety the Reformed Church brought most of its missionaries in Free China out of the country on furlough. At war's end Bill Angus was one of only five Amoy missionaries remaining in China.

As the Mission restored its facilities after 1946, the Kuomintang-CCP conflict escalated into civil war. Luckily the armies fought far from the Mission territory, allowing optimism for evangelistic and humanitarian progress among returning missionaries and new recruits, and the rebuilding of schools and hospitals. While converts who had not fled from the Japanese to other countries were stalwart in their faith, new conversions and the ranks of the native clergy dropped off. Subsisting under fantastically mounting inflation consumed the populace in work and panic, driving preachers into more lucrative occupations and students away from theological education. Overnight, necessities once purchased with a single Chinese dollar were driven to the cost of thousands, then millions, in inflating postwar currency. The price of restoring China's infrastructure was said to be to blame.[19] But those in the know, including some missionaries in the cities, blamed Chiang's grafting generals and officials, and the corrupt bankers and industrialists who supported his regime.[20]

Inflation was one of the causes of the Kuomintang's downfall. Its war on the Communists was the other. As it had before the war, the Chiang-led Kuomintang lurched from crisis to crisis without ever firmly grasping the fabled opportunities therein. Chiang refused to make the democratic peace with the CCP urged on him by the U.S., which

19. Other causes of postwar inflation were the closing of defense industries and unemployment among demobilized soldiers, currency speculation, and the many foreign currencies brought into China by the world war. Jonathan D. Spence, *The Search for Modern China* (1990), 498.

20. Unlike the CCP, the Kuomintang offered the people no unifying agenda, and the untimely personal avarice of its members and supporters kept it from establishing one. Graft, or "squeeze," had been the way of hierarchical life since the mandarins. Chiang used it as a time-honored political tool to cement alliances: he subordinated warlords in part by permitting them to steal their own troops' pay. During the postwar inflation the financiers who had supported Chiang's rise were said to be his cronies in a scheme to defraud the public of their supplies of specie and stable foreign currency by encouraging its "patriotic" exchange for postwar dollars in the name of beating inflation. Varg, *Chinese, Diplomats, and Missionaries*, 297-298.

shortsightedly grew tired of funding his money-draining government. Like the dynasts and warlords before him, Chiang denied the people a constitution and parliament—reforms and uplift failed to come, though taxes and requisitions did. For two decades the Kuomintang ignored the masses, posturing as a still-new government fighting for its life against communism, a reflection of its moral stasis. The people instead wanted the peace and stability that civil war deprived them of. The CCP won popular tolerance by making land reforms where it held territory, by promising to materialize the chimera of economic parity, and by offering the masses a disciplined and penetrating involvement in government that appealed to both the intellectual and the ritualistic aspects of the Chinese character. Its military and propaganda campaigns took advantage of Chiang's anti-modernism in not extending responsive government beyond the village level; once the national contest was over the Communists would consolidate their authority through bureaucratic ubiquity.

Had Chiang's government been as omnipotent as it was corrupt, it might have held on. But by the summer of 1949 the Communist resurgence outfought the Nationalist armies—weary, ill-paid, undermanned, and apathetic—and brought down the Kuomintang. By the early fall Communist armies took Foochow and the cities of the Amoy Mission territory. Reformed missionaries were not alarmed at first—the experience of demanding or expecting U.S. military aid was unknown to them. Like the people of the Mission territory, they had known many years of Communist-Nationalist struggle without a decisive victory or a radical change of living conditions in Fukien. Even Mao's declaration of a new People's Republic transmitted only the prospect of having to work under a new Chinese government. The thirty-seven remaining Amoy missionaries resolved to stay in China as long as they were able to.

Initially the churches, schools, and hospitals continued as they had since the war—as did missionary activity—with some variations imposed by local officials. But soon government scrutiny descended on missions and churches. Officials interrogated missionaries about their work and associations, and their opinion of the government, often at exhausting length. Public demurrers were accepted graciously, but missionaries' private words and activities, and those of native clergy, were reported on by informers. Missionaries and clergy were cautioned not to address political subjects in their preaching. Native pastors were indoctrinated and required to open their sermons with lectures on communist ideology. Missionary travel was limited by refusal of travel passes, curtailing evangelism. Soon village churches were closed and the buildings adapted to state use, though limited Christian meeting was tolerated in private homes, or "house churches."

Gradually and thoroughly—as Angus records in his poem "An Exceeding Weight of Glory"—Communist authority infiltrated the lives of the people. At the hospitals and schools, once-minimal government control advanced to harassment of staff and a freezing out of missionary involvement. Patriotic workers' associations were organized for all trades and callings; their members criticized and reported others who appeared not to measure up to the ideal of enthusiasm and commitment to revolutionary principles. Professionals, leading citizens, and even the church elders and clergy at Tong-an were sent to Foochow for ideological indoctrination—"brainwashing," in period parlance. Many—like the teacher described in "The Learner"—returned schooled in how to pay lip service to the new regime, and warned missionaries to keep their distance from their former Chinese friends. Others wholeheartedly embraced this political-economic regimentation of popular opinion just as they had the old ways of ostracizing non-conformists, and became fatal enemies of those who did not rigorously follow the Party line. Members of workers' associations publicly denounced colleagues who were not "progressive" thinkers—these were replaced, or arrested, tried, and executed as is the school superintendent in the poem "Tribute to the Sims." Communism not only supplied the long-sought panacea of political modernism, but satisfied the desire for enforced social conformity as well. Where the newspapers were not filled with political propaganda, they were filled with public apologies by persons who repented their earlier politically incorrect thinking. The officials who compelled their statements were likewise under Party scrutiny.

At Leng-na, where the Anguses were stationed, meetings of the church Classis, or governing body, were forbidden. Street preaching was disallowed, and increasing restrictions reduced church activity to a single Sunday service held in changing locations, impossible for the congregation to keep up with. Angus, like other missionaries, stopped preaching at services to avoid tainting the Leng-na congregation with his foreign presence. At the end of his time in China, he was unable even to deliver the opening benediction, as infiltrators of the congregation shouted him down as a foreign "warmonger" because of U.S. involvement in the Korean conflict.

The Korean War and American attempts to keep the PRC from seizing Formosa (the island of Taiwan, where Chiang's government had fled) brought mounting anti-foreign feelings that convinced missionaries to apply for exit permits from China. When the government froze American bank assets in retaliation for a like action in the U.S., missionaries like the Anguses were reduced to selling their personal possessions. Exit permits for Amoy missionaries were issued gradually throughout 1950 and 1951 on a case-by-case basis, which allowed review of those who might be arrested as agents of foreign imperialism. One Reformed missionary was accused and publicly tried, then released after brief imprisonment. Protestant and Catholic missionaries elsewhere fared less well, and suffered lengthy incarceration alongside native pastors brutally treated for refusing to tailor their faith to the Communist dogma. Soon the Party line was that American missionaries had been from the first collaborators in an imperialistic scheme to Westernize China. Bill and Joyce Angus—she had earlier evacuated their two sons—were allowed to leave in the Easter season of 1951. They were next stationed in the Philippines, like other old China hands who took assignments in neighboring Asian countries, ready to return should the Communists be overthrown.

The People's Republic guaranteed freedom of religious belief in a 1954 constitution, but made no guarantee of freedom of religious *observance*. Buddhist, Taoist, and Muslim assemblies and worship buildings were targeted for persecution along with Christian congregations and churches. During the Cultural Revolution (1966–1976), Mao allowed the youthful Red Guards to terrorize their religious elders into demonstrating total devotion to the state, and the closing or destruction of almost all places of worship followed. After Mao's death and the show trial of the "Gang of Four," said to be corruptors of the People's Revolution, temples, mosques and churches began to reappear, backed by constitutional reforms in 1982. Many Christians, especially in rural areas, preferred to worship in private homes—a perpetuation of the "house churches" that Angus visited at missionary outstations that could not sustain chapel buildings, and which sheltered underground congregations in the first two decades of communist rule. Such worship can partake of the merits and the risks of an unsupervised folk Christianity; it may also represent the achievement of a truly indigenous theology, which one Reformed Church missionary exiting China considered its ultimate goal.[21] Or it may be doctrinally suspect and politically subversive, as the present administration regards it.

Today the house church movement has colonized the cities, with unauthorized churches opening in homes, apartments, and office space. Some are so well congregated as to develop their own social programs—including missionary activities—attracting official disfavor. Reaction to the movement, and to other spiritual developments over the last decade, has been oppressive. Arrests were made—almost ceremoniously—during President George W. Bush's 2002 visit, and imprisoned Catholic bishops were notoriously refused release. The spring of 2011 brought extensive government sanctions against dissenters, with house church members harassed, beaten, evicted from their sacral spaces, and denied contact with world churches. Threats of job loss or labor camp internment press Christians to join registered and monitored churches. The ideological dynasts of the Central Committee scatter and imprison native Christians along with rights activists, liberal lawyers, democracy

21. Gordon J. Van Wyk, "Missions and Nationalism," *Western Seminary Bulletin* (1952), 8.

bloggers, and practitioners of Falun Gong spirituality.[22] When seen in this company, it is tempting to call Chinese Christianity a search for both modernity and the eternal—and faith a part of a quest that began with the desires for national identity and international prowess. As such, Christianity is not a contradiction to communism, but communism's competitor.

An Old Footlocker

I encountered William Angus's poetry while working as an archivist at the Joint Archives of Holland, at Hope College in Holland, Michigan. I arranged the several typescripts of a donation of his unpublished verse into the existing William R. Angus, Jr. Papers, one of the many Reformed Church missionaries' collections held there. The donation arrived in a battered footlocker, formerly a U.S. Army medical kit, that had been around the world during some of its most troubled times. Its present contents were an exciting find—engrossing and compelling narrative verse on China unknown to readers of poetry and history.

The earliest of the five newly donated editions was typed on sheets of rag paper with many strikeouts and typeovers (Angus was a two-fingered typist), and key-hits of irregular height that signal a much-traveled, much-repaired machine. I wish you could see them: the pages resembled nothing so much as dispatches from the front lines, which in more than one sense they were. I should rightly say "are," for these poems still possess an urgency of spirit, art, and documentation that marks them as communiqués from Angus's time to ours, and especially to the hearts of Chinese and Asian Christians. Their inherent currency moved me to subtitle this edition "Missionary Poems": the verse's mission to the faithful is yet real, and unobscured by time. Inherent in that mission is an authentic representation of place and period, admirable to the secular and religious reader alike.

Angus began writing his China poetry in 1931, while in the U.S. on furlough. Of his five editions, the two earliest are titled *South Fukien:*

22. Jacobs, Andrew. "Illicit Church Evicted, Tries to Buck Beijing." *New York Times* 18 April 2011: A4.

A Missionary's Miscellany. Angus divided each undated typescript into four volumes, attempting to collect the experiences of distinct time periods in twentieth century China. The volume titles introduced in the second edition—"Amoy and Points West," "The Mammon of Inflation," "The War Years," "Last Years"—show him moving closer to the epochal definitions of period that he would use last, and best.

The third typescript, dated 1954 and titled "Amoy and Points West," presents an undivided collection of South Fukien poems. This is the first of Angus's two attempts at assembling an edition of brief, marketable length. His fourth edition, called *Forty-eight Selections from South Fukien: A Missionary's Miscellany* (undated), is the briefest, and returns to a four-volume plan, but under pointed, modernistic titles: "Unrest," "Inflation," "War," "Communists." The selection of poems improves on the 1954 edition, and his arrangement of verses within volumes is at its most topical here.

Angus's last, and complete, edition, compiled in the U.S. during the 1980s, collected 664 poems written over five decades, revising many seen before. Angus divided the length into five volumes. "Change," the new first volume, addresses his early years among Chinese converts, focusing on native interpretations of Christianity and their self-governed church, and on the culture clash between the expectations of Westerners and the practices of the country. "Unrest," now the second volume, deals with life in South Fukien from the time of the Northern Expedition through 1936—the period in which regional bandits and Nationalist and Communist armies battled for the province. (Earlier editions commingle the poems of the "Change" and "Unrest" periods in one volume, of varying length.) "War" and "Inflation," as in their longer-titled originals, cover missionary and convert experiences through the Japanese invasion and the World War, and in the ruinous peace that brought little relief to the Mission territory, 1946–1949. "Communists," the final volume, details the "Last Years" of mission life, and the persecution of converts and former Nationalists under the new People's Republic.

I started reading where one might expect—in Angus's briefest edition. I remember vividly the first impression the verse made on me. Within the first seven poems read, I found "Good News," an annunciation heralding the Gospels' reception in village life, spoken by a convert preacher in the idiom of dynastic folktale. "That's your book-opener," I thought—a *bereshith*,[23] Hebrew for "the beginning" or "the origin." Two poems later, I read through "The Arm," and paused, as you well might. "Now here's a man with a foot in two worlds," I thought, and kept on reading. But I paused many times at the ends of Angus poems, as at country milestones. There is a journeying here, a mission seeking its fulfillment in the reader.

A great pleasure of reading the footlocker texts was experiencing Angus's uncompromising directness in addressing life and custom. This is manifestly not A Nice Missionary's Poetry. Its spirituality resists expression in homily and emerges instead from the discovery of moral certainties in mundane events—personal conflicts, doctrinal misinterpretations, unfairnesses, and everyday betrayals. (Some poems, such as "He Taketh the Wise," artfully recount a combination of these situations.) In the poems, moral resolution—sometimes, as China's peace declines, in a fatal encounter—often hangs on the pith of a simple utterance. Angus reports the bare words with which his characters respond to a situation, and the truth of the event seems to hang in the air before us, unheard by all but the narrator and reader. As in the Conrad of *Lord Jim*, or in Graham Greene's works, characters often condemn themselves by their own dismissive remarks. Thus the Kuomintang army commander in "A Call on the Fox" who puts off a pastor's attempt to convert him with a smile, saying, "I mean to. But, you see, I am so busy"—that is, busy eliminating bandits for the public good—doesn't fool the narrator or the reader. Both know he has been a bandit before and will be one again: he is simply liquidating the competition.

23. Some days later, when I cracked the complete edition to find out that Angus had chosen "Good News" to open the first volume, I felt myself the reductive shock of moral discovery that surprises the narrator of so many Angus poems. And so "Good News" came to open this edition.

The ultimate line of many Angus poems is an arch demurrer revealing the speaker's self-righteousness, callousness, or hypocrisy. So it is again in "Death of the Fox," after government troops kill Commander Keh (aka "The Fox") in battle:

> I saw the Fox's new home,
> Burned now and ruined. I asked them, "Why do that?
> If you get the man, you needn't burn the house."
>
> They said, "No one ever caught Keh before."

No one in Angus's verse need pretend. Yet there is a neutrality to Angus's moralism that admits sizable ambiguities. What are we to make of the last utterances in "Luck," "Cheaper," and "Safe"? Is the extreme devotion to their faith shown by the convert characters misplaced, even self-destructive—as individual interpretations of any faith can become? Other poems, in which the narrator confronts fear of moral indecision, hypocrisy, or worldliness in himself ("The Arm," the ironic "An Illustration," and "After the Looting," respectively), devastatingly indict the missionary.

Angus doesn't rely on surprise endings—there are precisely placed moral watermarks in the dialogue or events of his shortest verses.[24] Incisive quotations and last-line summations resist becoming the gimmicks of intentionality that he devalued in other poets because we feel them to be artifacts of human experience, each backed by a gallery of narrative detail. That detail is critical. After seasons of poetic imitation and influence, Angus took on himself the duty to be reportorial, "to set things down as they were, and not as I thought people at home would like to hear them." He explained in an early-1960s lecture series, typed up as "Talks on Religious Poetry."

24. The capsizing of the passenger boat in the brief "Rescue" becomes a tableau of moral failings, indelible as the strivings depicted in John Singleton Copley's Americanist painting *Watson and the Shark* (1778). Angus's verse, however, demonstrates that the soul is daily under duress, the sharks ever-circling.

> Most of my material I did not select or go in search of. I am not an inquisitive person and I hardly ever ask anyone a question. But I listened to people when they were talking together and often my mind would click and I would think, 'There's a story,' the way a minister might think, 'There's an illustration[.]' . . .I had to learn to see them, to see, as Henry James illustrated it . . . 'the *story* of it.'
>
> How can you tell the story of things as they are? [. . .] I decided not to round out plots or to improve on what happened, but to try to keep it just the way I heard it. However, I would sometimes combine two similar stories, or telescope a narrative or add a symbol or a detail. [. . .] I did not go outside my own [mission] area. Although sometimes I heard good stories from the north, I resisted the temptation to use them. And I used only oral sources.
>
> How clever should you be? I try to play it straight.

Such an approach required denying his early artistic tendencies, and an amount of self-sacrifice. Angus was well read in novelists and poets popular in the previous century and during his lifetime, and he read many with an eye for their narrative terseness. Yet his early narratives were influenced by voluble poets John Greenleaf Whittier, Edwin Arlington Robinson ("Bewick Finzer" and the Annandale trilogy hold analogs to Angus's Chinese portraiture), and Robert Frost. The enamorment lasted only a few years in-country.

> Later I changed my meter and my tone. My wife still regrets this, for I became deliberately less poetic.[25]

25. Early in China, when called to compose hymns for translation, Angus noted that "[e]verything I began as a hymn turned out a lyric. My emotions became too involved and my verses lost the serenity they needed." He rationalized, "I am often afraid to trust my ear, but put more faith in my eye or my mind." Odd self-doubts, from a poet of allusive nature lyrics such as "Late March: West River Road" or "Valley

> ... I came to feel that [Frost and Robinson] were at times too consciously the poet, and put in poetic lines which, although beautiful enough, might better have been left out.
>
> [T]he poet must ask himself, 'What is my attitude toward my material, toward the people whose lives I am recording or portraying? What is the work I am doing or want to do among them?'

The reader might find the center passage disingenuous, along with the complaint that in "The Death of the Hired Man" Frost "dragged in" too many "details about making a load of hay." Angus's China atmospherics depend on just such naturalist evocation of eking out a living, or of losing one's livelihood. But he presents his details more baldly, not relying on lyricism for pathos when cataloging will do it. He distrusts the self-aggrandizement of the "poetic," and rejects it in his mission to simply report. Similarly, Angus wrote few "establishing" or linking poems to define the epochal structure he was seeking, fearing the risk of overdeveloping it thematically. The verse is less pretentious for the sacrifice, embodying immediacy rather than a "look back."

Studying E.A. Robinson, and schooled in Robert Browning—canonical by the time of Angus's youth—Angus writes dramatic monologue, spoken by a missionary locutor. Like the poet, his missionary might hear the events of a narrative from several sources, or from one, but almost always through conversing with natives in his pastoral duties, hearing their complaints, pleadings, and gossip. Only incidentally do we read a tale told by missionaries—"I didn't tell any stories about *them*," he noted. Angus's missionaries are faceless, and, though based on actual persons, are identified only by bare first names which resist any footnoting, as it is on the vitality of China and the

---

Landscape, Sin-kio," or the several others not collected here. Should we find Angus's reportage erring in the direction of the prose-poem, we should remember that he didn't trust the lyrical impulse applied to the striving of living persons, since he held much respect for striving. Plants and trees, after all, will bear up under any coloring you might like, and Angus saves his embellishments for them.

Chinese that his verse depends.[26]

Angus's locutor possesses a watcher's tentative stillness—never so much so as in "The Arm," where the missionary is so disturbed by a convert's confession of refusing schoolchildren shelter during an aerial bombing that his last line (" 'You could not have known,' I said") is not an expiation but a gasp of uncertainty and culpability. You are what you endure the hearing of, after all. Under less fraught circumstances, the quietus comes from the respect of a minister in a host country, or just the willingness to let life pass in peace—it can't help but be revelatory if you listen. Often an earthy knowingness emerges, as in "A Grandfather," where one stanza closes with a young woman denying that she could be in love with the title character, shuddering distastefully at his age. The next stanza, though, begins,

> And so they eloped. He left behind him a wife
> And four young children[.]

Angus dealt with sharpers and canters, lovers and thieves—all manner of sinner. But remember that he came late to evangelist ministry, wanting originally to be an expert farmer for China. Part of his knowingness developed with awakening self-knowledge, with addressing human need while overcoming uncertainty at being an ordained man. (The title of *South Fukien*'s first volume, "Change," seems more like a chapter heading to the life of the youthful missionary than to the lives of the beset Chinese.) His verse is weighted with apperception, with awareness that he is a much-watched watcher in this land. His circumspection wards off precipitate moralism, threat of dishonor or worse—or merely the evils of being a bad guest. This missionary is not enthused with his own righteousness, and so not with others' claims to it.

26. To know how accurately and without effect Angus renders the feeling and characterization imparted in simple sentences of Chinese common speech, compare his character dialogue with the words of contemporary Chinese interviewed for Ian Buruma's *Bad Elements: Chinese Rebels from Los Angeles to Beijing* (2001). Older dissidents' complaints against callow younger Chinese echo those of the pastor in "Not Ashamed." Buruma, 21, 73.

At times, as in "The Arm," and in "The Shooting" and "Hush!" we glimpse in Angus the displaced Westerner of Greene's fiction, around whom the landscape may suddenly grow very wide, or very close, and to whom a destiny may be imparted in the glances and motions of the natives. As in Greene, recourse is made to naked prayer—and so the layered outrage of the lines of "Good Friday,"

> When lie and callous lust become the fashion,
> When cruelty comes surging in like ocean,
> When in my heart as well hate would take station,
>
> Then I find good
> Thy poured-out blood

may have the sound of the English metaphysical poets, but also that of their contemporary interpreter T.S. Eliot. Similarly, "After the Looting"—my favorite Angus work—has the shorter line and spare stanzas of John Donne in "A Hymn to God the Father,"

> Sorry I am and sore,
> Not for my losses,
> But I shall do again
> What I repent now[,]

yet some of the apocalyptic urgency of Eliot's "Ash Wednesday":

> Send me Thy Spirit, Lord—
> Often so glibly,
> Often so fearfully
> This have I asked Thee.
>
> What if He come like flame,
> Making me stranger to
> All the sweet lusts of life?
> Still I must ask it.

It is no accident that these are the most modernist poems in Angus's work: a man being honest with God will speak in the language of his times and hope he is understood. The English influences join him to a moral tradition as old as the ballad of the Rood. But the brutal honesty within his rhetorical craft transcends influence, as Eliot said achievement within context does in the true poet [27]

"Someone Else, Not Me," which closes this edition, ends on a note that may seem anti-climactic and overly terse, as Angus and his wife meekly sail away from Communist China:

> So we went. One policeman
> Kept talking along in Mandarin, I nodding my head.
> "Do you understand me, pastor?" he asked. He smiled.
> "I'm afraid you don't."
>
> He spoke slowly then, and together
> We worked out the arrangements for our exit.

Yet the flatlined voice, and the narrator's mute acceptance of the policeman's uncomfortably complicit question, express consummately the numbness devouring the missionary, who must desert the people, experiences and service of the years that preceded this poem. The title refers to the words by which St. Peter denied knowing Jesus on the night of His arrest. Angus takes the apostle's burden upon himself; the moment, weighty and heart-felt, precludes question of presumption. One couldn't close a rich history that, in fact, ended in just such a small and pitiless reckoning, in some more demonstrative way.

Like Peter's faltering, Angus's may lead to the coming of a greater glory. A quarter-century after leaving China the poet expressed hope for Christianity's future there, believing that communism—that alternate Western doctrine—had broken down the dependence on old ways that had been an obstacle to missionary efforts. One modern China-watcher notes that after disillusionment with communism as practiced, Christianity is now regarded as a desirably "modern" religion precisely

27. In "Tradition and the Individual Talent," 1919.

because of its heritage in Western faith—that of egalitarianism and compassion, perceived now as the true "political correctness."[28] These are two qualities of the verse you are about to read. Publicity, a character in Angus's favorite Graham Greene novel reminds us, can be an acid test for virtue.[29] Angus's work deserves the test, in our time.

What Is Owed

In editing *South Fukien: Missionary Poems 1925-1951* I tried to combine the best of the poet's intentions for a published work. Through the years, he shaped a periodic record of Chinese life, less a short-story collection than a verse novel. I followed the best of his leads, keeping the twelve-poem per volume structure of his *Forty-eight Selections*, but adapting it to the five historical divisions of the poet's complete edition, with its evocative volume titling. I retained thirty-one of his forty-eight choices, and introduced twenty-nine poems collected elsewhere. In his experiments at arranging individual volumes, Angus was not shy about moving a verse with few temporal anchors from volume to volume for effect, and I went as far as he had gone over the decades. I studied his sequencing and juxtaposing of his own poems and tried to work in that spirit, while keeping in chronology poems that overtly or tacitly address historical events. I line-edited him, occasionally substituting an earlier and more pungent rendering for a later, and modified or trimmed some stanza structure for effect. I hope I made the alterations that I would offer a living poet, while observing the qualities that make Angus yet a "living" poet.

The Joint Archives of Holland at Hope College makes the texts of all of William Angus's poetry available to literary and historical researchers, and holds two 1976 interviews with Angus that were invaluable to this introduction. They are kept in the Old China Hands Oral History Project Collection, whose other missionary interviews,

28. Julia Ching, *Probing China's Soul: Religion, Politics, and Protest in the People's Republic* (1990), 142.
29. *A Burnt-Out Case* (New York: Viking Press, 1961), 131.

and photographs, will be of equal interest to scholars. My thanks to Geoffrey Reynolds, Executive Director of the Joint Archives, for his keen assistance.

John Lawson, Professor of English at Robert Morris University, reviewed the edition and made helpful emendations and suggestions—out of his regard for poetry, and in memory of a missionary ancestor beheaded by Chinese bandits in the mid-1920s.

David Angus authorized this collection of his father's work and made many wise and valuable contributions to it. Thank you, David, for your confidence in the project.

One owes a debt to what one loves, even to literature and history for the pleasure and enlightenment they bring. I am thankful that William Angus's verse is added to the sum of the things to be repaid.

David Andrews

South Fukien
Missionary Poems
1925 –1951

CHANGE

"Measure it every which way and keep on measuring . . ."

Good News

Said the preacher at an evangelistic meeting,
"The sea is three hundred thousand feet deep; how, then,
Can you sound it with a thirty-foot bamboo pole?
The riches of the Gospel are inexhaustible;
How, then, can I tell you about them in one small hour?

"This Gospel is not believed by stupid people,
But by people whose bones are heavy, whose heads are round.
Their bones are very heavy and their heads are round, round, round.
They believe the Gospel because it is the Word
Which brings salvation to a sinful world.

"The Gospel. What does it mean? It means good news.
Let me illustrate with a story. Years ago in Chuanchow City,
At the beginning of the Manchu dynasty it was,
A man was unjustly imprisoned. It happened, however,
That while in jail an old acquaintance of his,
Surnamed Li, Li Kiu-ngaw, returned to Chuanchow for a visit.
He had risen to eminence and was then prime minister.
The wife sought out her husband's old acquaintance
And, falling before him, begged him for friendship's sake
To secure her husband's release. He would not promise,
And sadly she went away.

"But Li called to him
One among his bodyguard and said to him,
'Take two men and go measure the prison gate,
Measure it every which way and keep on measuring
Until someone comes out and asks you what you are doing.
Then say to him these words . . .' And Li instructed him in
Just how he should answer.

"The men went out to the jail
And measured the great gate's height and breadth and thickness,
Measured the gateway slantwise, measured it around,
Measured the gateway crosswise, measured it up and down.
The guard went and told the warden, and at last
The warden came out to ask what they were doing.
'Our master, the prime minister, is in town,'
The leader replied, 'and he has a friend here in prison,
So-and-so, an old friend of his boyhood days.
He expects to come and visit him tomorrow,
But sent us first to measure the width of the gate
To see if his great chair which requires eight bearers
Will be able to enter.' And then the men departed.

"The warden shook with fear. He called the guard
To bring forth the prisoner, shaved the man's face and head,
Clothed him in new garments, and set before him
A bowl of eggs and noodles. He prayed the man
Would not take offense at him the warden, for
He had but done his duty. He then released him.

"And so the prisoner had his liberty.
Was that good news? And so it is with the Gospel."

Luck

"It's bad luck to do business on Sunday," said our visitor.
"I know, because I used to keep my shop open.
I didn't want others to take away my business,
Especially on market days. I went to church, sure,
But someone stayed in the shop to wait on the customers.

"I went on like this for three years and my business got worse,
Worse all the time. I couldn't find out the reason.

So, I said, 'Lord, I'm going to close on Sunday,
And I pray Thee to make my business good again.'
It isn't much better, but now I'm with the Lord
Instead of against Him."

"He's right," said one of the elders.
"Two weeks ago the Soa^{n}-sia^{n}[1] market day fell
On a Sunday, and just when I needed to go
To get some stock for my stall in the Ka-Tang-khi^{n} market.
(A friend of mine in Soa^{n}-sia^{n} gets my supplies.)
But I stayed at home. And that day the man I go with
Was held up by bandits and all of his money was taken.
I said to my boy, 'There's a lesson for both of us.
Don't try to do business on Sunday or God will correct you.' "

A month later he ran into bandits himself.
"Was I lucky!" he said. "I had just paid a debt,
And all I had left was a two-dime piece. The men
Were so angry that one of them knocked me down with his gun-butt.
I feel more and more that the Lord takes care of His own."

He Taketh the Wise

"No," said the old preacher, "you can never tell
Who will turn out to be the finest Christian.

"There used to be a man up in Leng-soa^{n},
A simple fellow who gathered fuel for a living.
He heard the Gospel. A happier man alive
You never saw. He praised God night and day.
He had to work hard, too, to make ends meet.

1. See note 16 above for explanation of the use of the superscript *n*.

"Well, the congregation decided to build a new church
(That's the one they have now that was just repaired),
And this man was so happy you couldn't hold him.
He pledged them fifty dollars and paid it down,
Money he'd saved up cash by cash for years,
Pleased as could be to give it to the Lord.

"The consistory had some sharp old fellows those days.
They said, 'Here's a good man. Let's get him as caretaker
Before the church is built, pay caretaker wages,
And let him do day labor. We'll save that way.'
They hired him. *He* thought his cup was full.
He was so proud because they'd chosen him
To help build the Lord's house and to care for it.

"Then he learned to read the Bible. He loved it so,
He used to sit while the tears ran down his cheeks
And tell how thankful he was he'd learned to read
So that he could know God's Word.

"So he stayed on
As caretaker at four dollars a month for years.
And then he came with another fifty dollars he'd
Saved the same way and gave it to the church.
'I'm happy,' he said to me. 'Oh, I'm so happy!'
The tears ran down his cheeks. 'God's good to me,'
He said, 'He made it possible for me
To give a hundred dollars to the church;
It's more than I ever dreamed, the joy of it.
Oh, every day brings with it some new blessing.' "

Cheaper

I told Uncle John about our meetings. He said,
"Whenever I hear a preacher tell the villagers,
'Christianity is cheaper,' I think of a man I knew.

"He made his living selling little pigs.
He was withered, scrawny, poor—how poor he was
I can't describe. 'His living,' I called it, but he
Would have said simply that he 'passed the days'—
Survived. Yet, all but starved, he was a man
Who had the Spirit's fire in his heart
And a consuming longing for God—our God,
Though I don't believe he had ever heard of Him.

"He worshipped at the altar of his clan;
Tapers and incense and the rest he gave
Gravely, devotedly, out of inner need.
For he denied himself one meal each day
And on the first day of each month he spent
A dollar for the comfort of his gods.

"One day a Chinese pastor came and preached
The Gospel to him, and the man believed.
Convinced, he then renounced his fathers' halls,
The banks of dusty tablets and the dark
Bewhiskered images, the wayside shrines
To Buddha, and the cryptic Taoist scrawls
Which hung above his door, to be a disciple
Of Jesus Who was crucified for him.

"The first day of the month he came to them
And offered them his dollar. And they stared,
The deacons, at this man who freely gave
As Christ to him was freely given, though

He seemed to them to be near starvation. One of them
Went and called the elders (there was no pastor then)
To consider the case and see what could be done
For this poor man who was giving too much.

" 'Brother,' they said, 'you are a Christian now.
You don't need to give the church so much.
The images and Buddhas would take all,
But forty cents' small money is what we take.
It does not cost so much to worship here.'

"He was a simple man, and as they said
He did. Perhaps it didn't work out so badly.
He had more rice. He needed it, for soon,
He gravely, mutely wasted to his death."

Behold My Lord

Said Uncle John, "I loved our grand old man
Because he was so good. He wrote a hymn,
'Behold my Lord,' about our Savior's death
As he sat one day and thought of Christ's love for us all.

"I tried to translate it once. It was too compact.
I had to leave out too much, so I gave it up.
'Let us spend our lives trying to pay Him back,' his hymn ends,
And his life expressed loyalty and gratitude
Free from self-seeking and pettiness. He cared only
To serve his Master and to bring His kingdom here.

"Our Lord's death moved him deeply. He spoke of Him
In utter humility and with tears of gratitude.
My first year out he administered communion
At Synod, and I remember him on that day,

How the tears streamed down his face as he spoke to us
Of the love which moved Christ to die for sinful men.

"In his church the communion service is holy communion.
Each member rises to take his bread and wine,
Both hands extended, head bowed in acknowledgment.
They know what Sacrifice means. The old man has shown them."

Holdout

The burden-man carried my burden into the chapel.
We sat drinking tea with the preacher. I said to the man,
"You used to go to church. Why don't you go now?"

"I'm a called-in man. My father-in-law won't let me."

"But he's a Christian himself," I said.

"Sure he is.
Now don't ever let him know I told you this,
Or he'd take it out on me. He won't let me go
Because he says there'd be nobody left to burn incense
Before the tablets. He says we can't all be Christians;
Somebody has to stay out to make the offerings."
"He doesn't know what Christianity is," said the preacher.
"Why do you listen to him? He can't make you do that."

The man bobbed his head, but continued.
"I went to church before he adopted me.
And I go now if there's something special on,
But whenever he catches me he bawls me out.
If he were my own father, then I could say,
'You do your way and I'll do mine.' But I'm adopted,
And if I disobey, the neighbors will criticize
And say I'm not a good man, not worth adopting."

A Grandfather

When we were starting the girls' middle school at Leng-na,
We found a man, a member of the local church,
A local man, a college graduate,
An ex-teacher and ex-official. He became
The principal's right-hand man. When you're starting a school,
It's so easy to make mistakes, to ignore someone,
Or give offense in some other way. We were saved
From these pitfalls by Chiu; he knew everybody.
He saw officials, landlords, contractors, kept the wheels moving.
And he was a good teacher. He was invaluable.

His daughter died in Hong Kong. He went down there
And brought back his grandchildren. It was on his way home
That he met a former schoolmate, also a teacher,
And recommended her to teach in the school.
She was a Christian, a plain, serious woman,
Faithful, a good teacher herself. After a while,
However, the faculty noticed that she and Chiu
Were going around together. He sometimes took her
Out to one of the restaurants for a meal.
The principal's wife cautioned her to be careful,
But she pulled down her mouth and said, "He's a grandfather."

And so they eloped. He left behind him a wife
And four young children (the three elder ones were married)
And the two little girls he had brought back from Hong Kong.
From Changchow he wrote a letter to his wife,
Said he didn't consider himself really married to her,
Their marriage had been arranged for them by their parents.
But now he had met the girl he loved, and she
Was his true bride in the sight of God. His fields,
His property he gave to his wife for her support.

We were dumbfounded. The wife was raging mad
And went to the pastor and the consistory
To insist that he should be disciplined. They agreed,
And a meeting was held to decide how to handle the case.
His letter to his wife was offered as evidence;
He was an adulterer.

On the other hand,
Before he could be disciplined it was necessary
To remonstrate with him and ask him to repent.
It would have to be done by letter. But who could write
That kind of letter to him? Even the preacher was not
His equal in learning. They called in the principal
And asked him to write a letter suitable to them,
Which he did. They had a copy made for posting,
Stamped it with the official stamp, and sent it.

Chiu's reply was defiant. The letter, he told them,
Though in different hand, was unmistakably
The principal's letter. He recognized the style.
As before, he asserted that he had not committed
Any breach of morals. He did not love his wife.

As a first step, they suspended him. He and the girl
Were a long time unemployed, had a pretty hard time.
At first they attended services at Tang-poa^n-au,
But they didn't feel comfortable there, and began to go
To the Little Flock. If we can believe his letters,
The evangelist there reassured him, said his sin
Was minor compared to such a sin as Pride.

It was hard on his wife, but harder on his daughters,
Girls in their teens, one engaged to be married.

Girls

"Yes," said the woman, "She's a pretty child,
My youngest, and I love her . . . Yes," she said,
"They wanted me to drown her, but I saw
Those two little bright black eyes look up at me
As she was at my breast, and I wept and wept.
I couldn't drown her though we had no food.
Now I am glad, for I have heard the Gospel,
And our whole family has received God's Grace.

"That friend of mine I brought to the Woman's School
Has had six children. Two of the three boys died.
One girl she was able to give away, and one died.
The last she had to drown, they were so poor.
She held it under water in a pail—
That is the usual way out where we live.
Oh, no! She'd never do it now any more—
She cries sometimes when she thinks of her little girls.
But she still has a son—and when she can,
She'll take a girl into the house for him."

Safe

"Twenty-nine children baptized in one morning," I said,
"That's a record."

"There'd have been more," said the pastor,
"Two girls, but the mothers wouldn't let them be baptized.
They're going to give them away to heathen families."

"They're church members—"

"Yes, but still they don't understand.
When I was first married I did the same thing myself.
In the first three years my wife had three children, all girls.
She couldn't suckle and care for all three of them,
So I took the second and gave her away to some neighbors—
Good people, but heathen. They said she might go to church
When she was old enough. Ai-yah! I never thought
That a few years later they'd move to another village
Where there wasn't a church. We felt badly about it.
We prayed for her, and many a time I walked
Twenty miles, took a day off to see her and teach her
So she could be saved.

"She died when she was sixteen
And then I felt better. I knew she was safe with God."

Big Sister

As a little girl, bright-eyed, intelligent,
A missionary first saw A-chi. Later on
He arranged with the girl's foster parents to let her come
To the Girls' School. A-chi was shy, but merry,
And a very good student. Teachers and girls all liked her.

Her foster parents had bought her as a baby,
Had planned to have her marry their eldest son,
But he died while she was at school. So she stayed on.
Ten years went by. She became, first, one of the teachers,
Then dean of the school.

Suddenly, she was summoned
To return home and marry the second son, Ka. He was younger
Than she was, much younger, like a little brother.
They didn't want to marry. The old folks insisted;

They wanted to see Ka married before they died.
"What a shame!" said Bess. "He's just an ignorant farm boy."

A-chi married him. She taught in the school as before,
But now she was working to get him an education.
He went through lower middle, and then decided
To study to be a preacher. Three more years.
And then he had a church, and she went to join him.
They had no children.

They could get along
On the salary he got, but she had some debts
From the days when she was supporting him in school.
So, after a year at the church with him, she returned
To the school again, to teach for another year.
A cousin of his, a young girl, kept house for him,
But he petted the girl so much some church people objected,
And A-chi had to drop her work and go back again.

They adopted a child. Then A-chi began to have fever.
Perhaps she had worked too hard those years at school.
At any rate, she developed tuberculosis.
She went with the child back to her husband's village,
To her foster parents, to rest. The child gave her no rest,
So they sent him back to Ka. I'd visit A-chi
Whenever I passed through. She was different then
From when I had known her before, so full of worries
About the child, her husband, and herself,
About their finances, the money they owed.

Ka had been a good boy. His family wasn't Christian,
But he had been converted by his wife.
He was independent, thought things out for himself,
And made a good preacher, well above the average.
But he was tempted again. The child tied him down,

And one of the elders offered his servant girl,
A quiet, hard-working girl named Gek-a (Jade)
To go there daytimes and care for the child. Then someone,
Passing by and looking in the window,
Saw Ka with the girl on his lap, laughing and holding
And kissing her. There was a lot of that,
And because of the gossip the elder, becoming angry,
Began to mistreat the girl and to insult her.
She told Ka about the elder, how he'd take
The rice bowl away from her, or lock up her bedclothes
And shout at her, "Why don't you go sleep with the preacher?"
They had a consistory meeting to question Ka;
He denied that he had done anything wrong—and resigned.

He went to the city, made certain arrangements there,
Came back to the house of a friend and spent the night.
The friend said later that Ka was very restless,
Couldn't finish his food, paced the floor for hours
Far into the night. The next afternoon the girl
Came out to meet him. They went to her parents' house
And stayed the night. Then he took her to the city
And the day after that they disappeared.

The elder,
Enraged when he heard that his servant girl had eloped,
Sent a message to all the churches
Setting forth the case against Ka in unrestrained language.
He privately threatened to sue Ka and make him pay
A good price for the girl, or have him jailed.
But he himself was known as a rather sharp dealer,
And someone said, "If you let your chicks run loose,
You can't complain if a hawk should come and snatch one."

Ka and the girl passed through our town, didn't stop
Or call on anyone, but so it happened

They were hailed by his cousin, the girl who'd kept house
For him before. She was washing clothes in the river
And saw them crossing the bridge. They went right on
And didn't answer. After a short sojourn
In another town, he took the girl to his home
And they settled down there with his wife. He got a job
In the village school. His people thought nothing of it.
His father had had two wives and a brother had two.
They thought he was pretty clever to get her for nothing.

His home was in our district. One day, on our way
To attend some evangelistic meetings, the preachers
Began to discuss the affair. "Can't we fix it up?"
Asked one of them. "The girl could go back and say
She had gone with him to help take care of his wife."
"I've a better idea," said another. "Let her go
To the Woman's School for a term here and then go back.
She could say she went with him to visit his wife
And then decided to go to the Woman's School."

"Would it be true, though?" I asked. And another said,
"It makes no difference anyway. She won't go back."

Of course, the matter came up when Classis met.
The elder sent in a strongly worded letter
And the consistory asked the Classis for action.
Ka was dropped from the roll of preachers, and other districts
Were notified so they would not employ him.
His own church was instructed to discipline him—
And someone gave the whole thing to the newspaper.

A month later on my rounds I went to see him,
And the last was what hurt him most. To be crossed off,
Or suspended, excommunicated!—that was proper.
That had to be done. But to write it up in the papers,

He thought, showed malice on the part of someone.
"Tell him," he named a name, "he didn't need
To offend me as deeply as that. Now everyone
Says to me, 'I see the church took away your position.'
How do you suppose I feel?" He began at that
To tell me his side of the story. "It's not all my doing,
It takes two coins to jingle. More than once
The elder told me, 'Your wife will never get well.
When she dies I'll give you this girl here for a wife.'
Now he says *I* am the one who said that to the girl.

"You may think I've lost my religion to do this thing.
Before God I say I revere Him as before.
I took the girl away from them to protect her.
I had to do it—he treated her so badly.
She used to come to me weeping and tell what he did,
How he refused her food or a place to sleep . . ."

The man who had come with me was unimpressed.
"A funny way to protect the girl," he said; and,
"He's like Adam. He blames everything on the woman."

Ka had been to see us at the church. Now we went to the house
To see the women. He followed us there, however,
And what they said to us was in his presence.
The upstairs was one long room. A-chi was lying
On her bed in one corner. The girl was sitting
On her bed in another. After our greetings
We sat down near A-chi. Her eyes were filled with tears.
"If the people of that church," she said, "had shown
A particle of love, this needn't have happened.
Why didn't they talk to him in a spirit of trust?
Why didn't they see that Gek-a was treated fairly?
I don't care for myself. I'm as good as dead:
My body is dead; all I have left is a voice.

But the Lord's work must suffer because of this."

"He threatens to sue," said Ka, "But all we need to do
Is to have Gek-a put a notice in the paper
Saying she came of her own free will."

I spoke
To the girl. She wept and said, "I'll never go back
To that place after the way they treated me."
She had always been a girl of good reputation,
Good-hearted, sensible, active in church work.
She and A-chi seemed to like each other. In fact,
I thought A-chi looked stronger and happier.

I was assigned to another district. Three years passed
Before I went to see them again. A-chi was up,
Not entirely well, but well enough to teach school
And lead the church services. Ka gave her his help
In the church work, but he did not lead a service.
Gek-a, washing clothes in the brook, called a greeting.
A baby was strapped to her back. She'd miscarried,
But recently had this child, a girl.
Ka stood with me outside the church that evening
And asked for news of his friends and former colleagues,
Spoke wistfully of church work and church problems.

A-chi took a walk with me after church next morning.
She said, "I know what Ka did wasn't right.
It was wrong. I don't defend it. But it turned out
All right. I would have died except for Gek-a.
She's a good girl. She was willing and cheerful
Right from the start. I was too weak to wash
Or do any heavy work, and she did it all,
Pitched right in, took care of the house and the child,
Took care of me. And she was always happy
And made me happy, and I began to get well.

But Ka isn't happy. I wonder, pastor, if you
Couldn't get him back his preacher's job again?"

"It can't be done," I said. "There's no use trying
As long as he lives with Gek-a." A-chi knew that too.
But she and Ka had not wanted to marry each other;
She'd always been like an older sister to him.
It was a relief to her that he had Gek-a,
And Gek-a was a good girl who loved her too.
They were all satisfied. Why couldn't Ka have his job?

An Illustration

He was trying to comfort a woman whose husband gambled.
"Long ago in Chioh-be there was a woman whose husband
Would keep her from going to church till she gave him money
For gambling. He was a rascal and sponged on her,
And she took in washing and mended clothes for a living.
But she was patient and prayed."

"Did her husband reform?"

"No. He died. And she became a Bible woman.
God opened a road for her that way." He caught himself.

"I was only using that as an illustration," he said.

Late March: West River Road

These are the days when in the temple groves
The luminous green of the liquid-amber tree
Stipples the darker green of fir and pine.
The new leaves of the kwa, ruddy and bright,

Obscure the older foliage and reflect
The soft gold of the sunlight through a haze
Of early mist.

These are the days
When on the hillside all the little pines
Raise yellow fingers Heavenward, when the gray
Cover of the last year's bracken is pierced and torn
As the new shoots uncurl and decorate
The somber hills, encroach upon the black,
Burned-over patches, and prick out with green eyebrows
The hard, unwinking eyes of winter graves.

These are the days when shining shrubs and trees
Flash from behind the tall brown river grass
And the dejected bamboos on the banks.
The bamboos are like pale and stooped old men;
They nod and sway and their yellow leaves droop sadly.

These are the days when along the hillside path
The flower buds of the bread-and-butter vine
Are little sprays of bubbles held above
The graceful downward sweep of the curved leaves;
When the white stars of the opening Cherokees
Give promise of the white cascade to follow
The long, slim canes down to the runnel's edge;
When the bomb in the heart of the thistle is ready to burst,
And still other flowers of tree and bush and grass
Are lovely images without names.

These are the days when on the farms the pink
Of peach and white of plum have dropped and gone,
When the bananas raise black and ragged arms,
When pineapple spears are yellow on the hill,
When the flame of the opium is quenched,

And the bald and blackened pods are scratched and scraped.
The winter crops are done.

                    These are the days
When cane and sweet potatoes are set out,
When flooded fields are plowed and harrowed, when
The green rice shoots are ready for a planting.

UNREST

"What if He come like flame? . . ."

Not Ashamed

When the Nationalists came through in '26,
The people were given Sun Yat-sen for their saint,
And his picture was in every public building.
We had plenty of meetings in those days. The boys
Marched off to this or that about every other day,
Were harangued to exhaustion. Many speakers were Reds,
Anti-foreign and also anti-Christian—
For Christianity was a "foreign religion,"
And Christians were "the imperialists' running dogs."

The town was plastered with slogans. Never before
Had we seen the like, though we saw enough of it later.
Anti-Christian posters were on all the churches,
And one of our pastors accused of pulling one down.
They led him off to a mass meeting in the park
And speakers howled themselves hoarse in condemning him
As a running dog and traitor. It happened that
They had taken a man who was very patriotic.
We had often heard him sound off against the foreigners,
The missionaries included.

"Shall we let him speak?"

Asked the chairman.

"Let him speak!" yelled the crowd, delighted.

They knew him.

"Yes," shouted the pastor, "I was a revolutionist
Before you were born. I'm being falsely accused
Because I'm a Christian. I never tore down that poster.
They pasted it too low and some child tore it down."
He climbed the steps of the platform as he spoke,

But as he reached the center the chairman seized him.
"Listen to him claiming to be patriotic
With never a bow to the portrait of our leader!"

"I'll bow to him," said the pastor, "let me talk."

"Down with the running dogs of imperialism!"
Shouted the men on the platform, and hustled him off.
They tied his hands and led him around the streets,
Shouting and waving banners. Boys pelted him,
Children ran screaming ahead to look at his face,
People piled out of their doors till the street was blocked.

Whenever the march was halted, there was a lull
As people asked what all the shouting was for.
That was the pastor's chance. In tones of thunder
He told them these men were trying to put him to shame
Because he believed in Jesus Christ as his Savior.
"But I'm not ashamed," he shouted. "He is the Savior,
And China will not be saved but through Him!"

He kept it up all afternoon. When they let him go
He stumbled back home exhausted, but game to the end.
He sipped his tea. "These youngsters," he said, "they have no roots."

Toast Refused

"You never drink wine," said the preacher. "That saves you trouble.
Let me tell you what happened to me one time at a feast.

"They put me at the first table with the commander,
And he insisted on having three of his women
At the table there with him. Of course they started drinking,
And one of those women got up and bowed and said
She would honor me with a glass. But I wouldn't drink.

The commander got up. His face became very fierce.
The way he looked at me just about curled my hair
And my heart began to pound. But a friend of mine
Stood up and told the commander I was a preacher
And didn't believe in wine drinking. On my behalf
He was happy to respond, and also to honor
The commander and his ladies with a glass.
So the commander relaxed and the thing passed off.
My friend came to see me later. 'What was the idea?'
He asked. 'You could have been murdered then and there.'

" 'I know,' I said, 'but I thought of people saying,
"The preacher was drinking with the commander's whore,"
And I couldn't drink; my body refused to move.
I thought, Let him cut my head off if he wants to.' "

Occupied Chapel

"Commander Tiu^n has taken the Lam-khi^n chapel,"
The letter read, "to use as a school for recruits.
The caretaker had to get out and rent a house
Across the street. Please come right up and help us."

At this time Tiu^n was beginning to feel pretty big
And had moved his headquarters down to Soa^n-sia^n.
The army, busy elsewhere, had taken him in again
And, for the same good reason, he had a free hand.
Immediately he began to lay big plans.
He combed the countryside for new recruits
And arranged to give them six months' special training
After the fashion of those higher up in his world.

Whether Tiu^n was a bandit or not was hard to say
At any given time, for, as you spoke,

He might just then be working out a deal
For government recognition, or hatching some scheme
To break away and run his own show again.
Bandit, soldier, he had been each many a time.
When he behaved, his little stamping ground
Became the safest spot in all the district.
But when he needed more cash than his levies brought in,
Folks with a little spare money had to be careful
Or they would be kidnapped. He deplored the thing—
Officially. They weren't his men, he said,
Or, if it was proved they were, he punished them.
But even the babies could add up that one.

Headquarters,
"At Soa^{n}-sia^{n}" then, were at Lam-khi^{n} most of the time.
Soa^{n}-sia^{n}, on the road between Changchow and Sio-khe,
Was too liable to be surprised by government soldiers.
Several times he collected money for a road
From Soa^{n}-sia^{n} up to Lam-khi^{n} and Tsun-tiu^{n},
But it was never finished. He wants to show progress,
But he wants to protect his main bailiwick from the troops.

My next trip out I went up to Soa^{n}-sia^{n} first.
The preacher there couldn't take me to see Tiu^{n},
Having crossed and offended him previously. A doctor,
One who attended Tiu^{n}'s men, agreed to take me.

"What do you want to do? Tell him to get out?"

"Yes," I said.

He sat a while silently, thinking.
"I'm afraid we'll have to be more politic.
We'll tell him we need the chapel for services
And the rooms for—well, anything you say.
We'll call on him after supper; daytime's no good.

He takes opium about midnight, doesn't wake up
Until eleven or noon. From then on he's busy
Seeing his men and settling his affairs."

Headquarters was one of a row of shops, but shuttered.
We passed the guard and climbed the stairs. "Stay here,"
The doctor said, "I'll go and talk to him first,"
He passed inside the partition. I heard the commander
Grunt with surprise and vexation. "I have no room,"
He kept saying, "I have to, I have no room."

The doctor called me in. Tiu^{n} was in his undershirt,
A big man with a mole in the middle of his forehead.
The three-eyed Tiger, they called him jokingly.
He received me pleasantly. We got along very well.
Over our tea he said he was pressed for room.
I told him what room we needed. He then agreed
To give us all we asked for, and said that he
Would remove his men in six weeks to new-built quarters.
We left.

I reported our visit to the preacher.
He was disappointed. He complained, "You were too easy.
Six weeks! He'll not get out of that place in six weeks.
He's planning to run his school for a whole year there.
No room! He has plenty of places to put his men in.
You should have asked him to go, let him take it or leave it.
We can't talk to him that way, but you're an American
And can use your foreign prestige to tell him things."

"Suppose I said to him, Get out, and he didn't do it?"

"All right, you should have said it and let him choose.
If he didn't get out, you could take it up in Changchow,
Or with your consul."

"No," I said, "I couldn't.
I didn't go to see that man as an American,
And you know the army can't do much with this fellow.
He'll tell them just what he told me—if he answers at all—
And do as he pleases. They have no hold on him."

"That's what *you* say," he grumbled, "not what *he* thinks.
He wouldn't listen to you if you weren't a foreigner."
The Lam-khi^n caretaker came to us when he heard of it.
He paled whenever we mentioned intervening.
"Just tell me when you do it, so I can run first.
The commander blames me now for your visit to him.
One of his men let me know it would be too bad
If Tiu^n were annoyed any more about this affair."

We didn't expect them to get out after six weeks.
The commander didn't intend to—but some men fell ill
And he moved them all out, at just the appointed time.
The Christians hailed it as proof of the power of God;
As in Moses' day, He was warning a stubborn ruler.
But Tiu^n was unrepentant like Pharoah. After
The New Year he occupied the chapel again.

Able to Give

The new street was put through by order of the commander.
It cut off half of the church. They had to meet
In an ancestral hall. One day the commander,
Riding horseback down the street, came upon an old man
Standing in front of the half-demolished church
With his eyes closed. "What are you doing?" asked the commander.

"Praying."

"Praying to whom?"

"Praying to God."

"For what?"

"A new church building."

The commander frowned.
He said, "Don't pray to God for that. Ask me.
I'll get you a piece of land for a new church building,
And you can go around and collect for the building itself."

He got the church a piece of land, not a bad piece,
And a good location. But the church didn't build on it.
After the commander had been driven out,
They returned the land to its owner. They were too wise
To build on expropriated land. They preferred to wait
More than ten years until God answered their prayers.

The Tiger's Things

When I let him in he was trembling with excitement;
He had taken the first 'bus down from Soa^n-sia^n
"The soldiers came into Lam-khi^n Chapel last night.
They took all my bedding and clothes and turned me out."
He was the caretaker.

"Just you?"

"No, they looted all the shops,
And they shot some people who they said were spies.
They are chasing the Tiger's men up into the hills."

"What have they done to the chapel?"

"I don't know.

I went out to sleep with the members late last night
And walked to Soa^{n}-sia^{n} early in the morning."

"What's the idea of a sudden attack like this?
I thought the commander was in the army again.
What has he done to make them go after him now?"

"I don't know," he replied. Later I learned from others
The commander had been in contact with Canton
And was involved in the brief southeast revolt.
"I've talked with our folks. Lau (the preacher in Soa^{n}-sia^{n})
Told me to ask you to help them. You're our moderator;
They want you to get them protection from the consul
So they won't be robbed as soldiers or shot as spies."

"The consul! That's no good these days. Besides,
None of the Christians live in the market village.
They're a mile away."

"Yes, but the soldiers might come,
And if they have them no protector they might be robbed."
His story sounded a little peculiar to me
But I promised to investigate. A few days later
A letter from Soa^{n}-sia^{n} said that all was well.

The commander was hunted by troops for several months.
His son and foster son were caught and killed,
His wife and concubine were put in prison.
Meanwhile the revolt was quashed; loyal Cantonese
Took over the whole of our district from the northerners—
And soon our commander was in the army again
With more power than before.

One of the Soa^{n}-sia^{n} Christians
Whispered to me as we drank our tea in his house,
"We ought to get a preacher for that station now.

The commander is feeling very friendly toward us,
For when he ran last spring he sent some . . . *things*
To be hidden out in our village, and when he returned
They were all there safe."

I'd have been scared, too.

The Tiger, the Bull, and the Fox

Tiu^{n}, Iap, and Keh, the Tiger, the Bull, and the Fox
Are the three main bandits in our immediate area.
We don't refer to them as bandits anymore.
They've established themselves; they each control a district.
The government calls them bandits at times, but then
At other times recognizes them as soldiers.
Fighting is followed now by negotiation.
Our friends don't call them bandits but commanders,
A fine, ambiguous title, always good.

The Bull
I have never met. His is the London Mission part
Of the Changchow Classis area, Phaw-lam and Giam-khoe.
Noel thinks he is the best man of the three.
"The other two are too clever. They get into trouble
Because they rob and double-cross everyone.
The Bull has more sense. He isn't too greedy.
He lets the people know what they can and can't do.
He takes their money, but gives more than he promises,
And gives real security—no double-crossing
Unless *they* do it, and that's the end of *them.*
They brag up there that no one dares steal a chicken,
And it's true. You can travel all over his district at night
And no one dares rob you.

"He looks after schools
More strictly than any Chinese I ever saw.
He gives bright boys a chance to go to college.
Some of his boys come here to our middle school.
His adopted son is here, a Christian boy.

"He gives me good advice about the preachers:
'Take that man out,' he says, 'he doesn't work.
Get us a man like that last man; he calls on people.'
He's almost too helpful for comfort at times. He says,
'What? Don't those fellows support the church? They have money.
Make So-and-so pay so much, and So-and-so.
Don't let them go without paying.' He knows them all.
He rules that county down to the smallest detail.
He rules them with his voice, I always say.
It rumbles along like thunder, and when he lets go
It paralyzes thought. They can't resist him.

"He and the Fox came along about the same time,
Took over counties next to each other there
When they drove the other men out, but look at the difference.
The Fox is up and down and in and out,
Keeping the people on edge with his endless schemes.
The Bull really tries to help the people; they like him,
And so the government soldiers let him alone.
Besides, he minds his own business, that is, his own county,
For everyone's business inside his own borders is his."

"The Tiger's at peace now, too," I said. "Last week
The pastor took me to see him. His wife's a member.
The pastor calls there when he makes his rounds.
He was telling Tiu^n that all his past misfortunes
(His son was shot, you know, and his wife thrown in jail)
Occurred because he lacked interest in the church.
It's hard, I suppose, to know what to say to a man

Who robs and murders and kidnaps as part of the game
And has your life in his hands if you chance to offend him.
The pastor did pretty well. The Tiger had a hard time
Before his friends the Cantonese came in."

"You haven't said much for the Tiger," said Noel, "unless
We count his church connections, but *our* men have those.
A brother, a wife, a foster son—funny thing,
Those links with the Church. But what does the Tiger do
Besides kidnap people? Does he run schools, build roads?"

"Collects the money for them," I replied.

"And what about the Fox?" asked Noel.

"He's crafty,"
Said Edwin, "and more dangerous than the Tiger.
Not to us, but to his enemies, I mean.
He has a sneaking affection for us, I think.
His brother's a Christian. The Fox went to one of our schools.
Our old pastor did him a good turn while he was there,
Rescued him when *he* was kidnapped by actors,
Remembered him from school.

"He learned that lesson,"
Said Noel. "He can do a fine job now himself."

"No, not that one," said Edwin, "a later lesson.
He was kidnapped again as a young man.
It cost his family everything they had
To ransom him. He said, 'I can play that game.'
He and two others ambushed some government soldiers
And got five guns. Soon he had half a county.

"Since then he's had many hard times and weathered them all.
Often troops have come in and tried to drive him out,

But he disbands his men and goes into hiding.
The county is pacified, the troops depart;
He reassembles his men, resumes control.
He was almost caught a year or so ago.
Some of his men turned traitor. The government men
Were a little above average. But he escaped,
Although he lost more than half of his rifles and money.
He has reestablished himself now, and I'm told
He is quietly removing his betrayers."

Black Bills

"Here," said the pastor laughing (we were out calling),
"Here is a man who knows all about black bills."

"I ought to," he said, "they handed me three last winter.
Though what money they think I have I'm sure I don't know.
Look at this house! The whole thing's falling to pieces.
Think I can rebuild? I've got brick stacked all around,
But I won't start so much as a wall 'till the country is quiet.
I'm three miles away from the market. I get no protection,
So I just lie low and keep still. My son has friends
Who go with a gang and they try to help me out.

"Well, the first two times weren't much. My daughter-in-law
Found the letters outside when she opened the doors in the morning.
The first was for thirty, the second for forty dollars;
I went to their camp and got off for ten each time
And that ended it. But the last one was something different.
Three hundred dollars! The leader was gone for a while,
Had run up to Ho-te, and this was his lieutenant acting.

"I went to see them. 'You've got to pay it,' they said.

" 'I haven't that much money.'

" 'Borrow it, then.
We need it.'

"I asked them to give me a little time
And then I sent word to my son. He was down in Phaw-ah
Where he worked for the man whose son was in the gang.
The son was the Number One's bodyguard. Well, the old man
Sent to his son and he got my news to the leader
Who told them to let me go this time.

"That was fine,
They let me go – but it cost me sixty dollars
To thank them for it. One of the gang came up
And told me what was expected: cigarettes,
Two hams, pillow cakes, canned fruit—sixty dollars worth,
And sixty dollars to me is no trifle to laugh at."
He sighed. "I tell you, living is tough these days."

A Favor

Said Hank, "As bandits go, our bandit wasn't a bad one.
He was cruel. He taxed heavily. He strutted.
He had all kinds of finery and a houseful of women.
But he was brave and able, and he wanted to help the people.
Sometimes he'd tell me some of his ideas.
'You Americans,' he'd say, 'how I admire you.
What a wonderful country America is. You do things.
You're always inventing. You're never satisfied with anything.
China's a stick-in-the-mud country . . .' and so forth.
And he would tell about the park he was going to make,
The roads he was building, the athletic field,
The wide streets, the big new market, the school.
But he was the one who was doing it, no one was telling *him*.
And he wasn't asking the people for help, he was taking it.

"He didn't care for the higher-ups, either. Once
Orders came down from somewhere, Foochow, I guess.
Someone he gave lip-service to. The orders
Were not to his liking. He slapped them with his hand.
'Orders are paper,' he said. '*I* cut the caper.'

"He sent a man over to our side one day, saying,
'I'd like to help you. Tell me what I can do for you.'

" 'Well,' I replied, 'we appreciate his great kindness,
But we don't need anything, don't expect to need anything
As long as this good government continues.
There's just one little thing I'd like to see done.
He's always shooting people just below our house
Down there in the graveyard, two or three a day.
If he could shoot them somewhere else, our children
Couldn't describe them to us all the time,
How they fell, and so on. It isn't good for them.
It makes them dream sometimes. You understand?
If he could do that little thing, I'd be grateful.'

"He shot them on the parade ground after that."

After the Looting

Sorry I am and sore
    Under Thy chastening,
Plundered of all I owned,
    Owing men money.

Sorry I am and sore,
    Not for my losses,
But I shall do again
    What I repent now.

There were the starving men,
There were the homeless,
Children too weak to walk,
Babies past crying.

"Help them," I often cried,
"Help them I cannot;
Like a dull heartache the
Thought of them wracks me.

"But I must pay my bills,
Finish the planned things,
Keep up the house and the yard,
Hold to our standards."

Money we spent for things,
Bright rugs and curtains,
Linens and finer stuffs,
Crystal and silver.

Books without end I bought,
Fondled the bindings,
Ranged them on my shelves,
Packed and unpacked them,

Read them and looked at them,
Babbled about them all;
No one need read a book
Once I had finished.

Ay, where the treasure is
There is the heart too.
And I have thought of it,
Scolded my folly.

"Yes, Lord," I often said,
"If these things hinder,

Teach me to let them go
        Or take them from me."

Now that they all are gone,
        Scattered and stolen,
Must we eat wind again?
        Buying, replacing,

I with my books and files,
        Joyce with her pictures,
I with my easy chairs,
        Joyce with her curtains?

What is a tithe of all?
        People are starving;
When they have nothing,
        Dare we have surplus?

Shall these men teach us love,
        Wake us to living?
Shall they with gun and torch
        Challenge our Gospel?

Close to earth's lowliest,
        There is our service;
Things are our instruments,
        He is our brother.

Send me Thy Spirit, Lord!—
        Often so glibly,
Often so fearfully
        This have I asked Thee.

What if He come like flame,
        Making me stranger to
All the sweet lusts of life?
        Still I must ask it.

The Arm

The 19th Route Army revolted in '33
In December, and on December 23rd
Nationalist planes flew down and bombed Changchow.

He came to me a few days after the bombing.
He came in silently with gray head bent, sat down,
Arranged his gown, put a hand upon each knee.
He spoke deliberately. "Pastor, you've known me
Ever since you came here. I have been in business
At the same place for forty years. I am known in town
As a man who is straight."

"Very straight," I said with a smile,
"Everybody knows that."

"I'll tell you plainly, pastor,
What's happened. Some people are trying to ruin me
By spreading reports about me. You know that a bomb
Fell into the street just opposite my shop
And killed three little boys from our primary school
On their way home for lunch." I nodded. "Well, they say—"
He sighed and wiped his mouth with a handkerchief. "Say
The boys ran into my shop when they heard the planes
And I chased them into the street." He began to shake.

"Let me tell you the whole story, pastor. How could I do that?
I shuttered the shop as soon as the warning sounded
And all of us sat in the back around the table.
We heard a big crash outside and we fell to the floor.
When we took down the shutters, there was a schoolboy's arm,
The uniform sleeve still on it, against my door.
The building across from me was a heap of rubble.

"I called my clerks and we helped to find the remains.

We didn't know who they were, but their people came
And picked them out. The police came, too, to check up.

"That is the true story, pastor. I know the parents.
I've been to see them, to see the principal, too.
I wanted you all to know the truth of the matter,
For people are trying to ruin me with their talk."

I reassured him. The lines on his face were deeper
Than ever I'd seen them before. He did not weep,
But his eyes were fixed in a stare. "Oh, did I do right?"
He whispered. "We put up the shutters so fast. We were scared,
We sat in the back. But should we have been such cowards?
That arm, flung across the street to my very doorstep,
Seemed to be knocking."

"You could not have known," I said.

Communists

Southwest of Changchow, southeast of Sio-khe,
Is a range of hills which runs into seven counties.
For centuries it has been used as a bandit hide-out.
Ever since the Reds came down in '32
A band of Communists has held the place,
Helped out by others opposed to Nanking's rule—
19th Route Army men, Cantonese sympathizers.
From time to time the soldiers try to surround them
But they've never succeeded. It's almost impossible
In those hills without overwhelming force.
Sometimes, though, fighting is hot and losses heavy.
The Reds once lost three leaders in two months.

In general, the Communists seem to keep track of the soldiers,
But the soldiers can't keep track of them. Where they'll break out

Nobody knows. There's Thah-tham, Phaw-ah, Siang-khe,
Lam-sin, Gaw-cha, even Am-au, Toa-khe on our side,
And as many more places down Changpu and Un-sio way.
We were talking it over two months ago in Lam-sin
Where some of the men had been carried off by the Reds
And held for ransom.

Pastor Tiu^{n} told his story.
"What the government's idea was no one knew,
But suddenly one afternoon in '35
They pulled every Nanking soldier out of Lam-sin,
Leaving only the home guard to defend the place.
At two in the morning the Communists came down.
They picked on the church this time and tried to burn it,
But failed because the benches were bolted together
And they couldn't pile them up to reach the rafters.
So they burned the school, the parsonage, and the church doors,
And carried off me, my wife, my youngest child,
And four girls who were living at the school.
One of the men offered sugar cane to my youngest,
But he wouldn't take it. 'You're a bandit,' he said to the man.
'No, I'm a Red soldier,' the man replied, and laughed.
They released my son and wife when they'd gone a ways,
And the girls, unharmed, at the top of the mountain. Myself
They took to their camp. They had forty people there
Sitting bound and shackled awaiting ransom.

"They took me to their leader, who questioned me
Minutely about my income, my work, my family.
'Are you against religion?' I asked him first.
'No,' he said. He was a man of thirty-odd,
A little fellow, returned student from Japan.
'We were three years ago, but now in Russia

They have religious freedom and so have we.'
'Well, that makes me feel better,' I said to him,
'For I am a Christian pastor and must confess it.
As to anything else, you're welcome to search all you want,
For I have no money or property.' It was true.

"God helped me in my answers. They sent men down
And inquired about me, but it all matched what I told them.
They made me write a letter to my church
And ask them to raise a five-hundred-dollar ransom.
I wrote it, but I added to my request
A promise to stay with them and work out the debt.

"I was up before the leader again two weeks later.
He wanted me to talk with him in English,
As if he didn't want his men to hear us,
But I said I hadn't had much English in school,
So we spoke in Mandarin. 'I read your letter,'
He said to me. "You promised your people you'd work
To pay them back that money. You didn't exploit them.
We don't make money out of other people either,
And we're not after men like you. I shall let you go.'
I was kept thirty days in all and then released."

"Did the leader live like the soldiers?" one of us asked.

"As to eating and sleeping, yes," Tiu^{n} said.
"He ate two meals a day along with the others,
And they each had one blanket a night.
But his clothes were better. He had a sweater and an overcoat."

"Did he try to convert you?" we asked him.

"Yes," he said,
"We had several discussions. He said the government
Represented the propertied classes and he the propertyless,
And the educated must help the ones who have nothing.

I said I agreed in aim but not in method;
I believed in changing man by love, not force,
By holding up before him God in Christ,
Christ crucified, dead, and risen again for me."

❂ ❂ ❂

One of the listeners chuckled. "My daughter-in law
Was captured last year, same time as the preacher at Tiu^{n}-law
On the Changpu side. They let her mend his gown.
One of his members had called him over to help,
Said soldiers were taking him. He went. It turned out
They were Reds and took him, too. Well, he wouldn't preach
Or talk about the Gospel, my daughter-in-law said.
And the leader said to him, 'Why don't you preach to me?
Pastor Tiu^{n} and I used to have some fine old arguments.'
He had to pay two hundred dollars to get out."

"And when my father was captured in Am-au," said a youngster,
"He said he was a Christian and right away they asked,
'Who's pastor at Lam-sin?' 'Tiu^{n} Beng-siu,' he said.
He got off for a hundred."

"That's funny," I said,
"The same thing happened when they captured Khaw at Chhiah-lau.
He said, 'I'm a preacher.' They said, 'Who's pastor at Lam-sin?'
And when he gave them details they let him go."

"As a rule, I don't think religion makes any difference.
They're after the clan elders, officials and gentry,"
Said the oldest of us who was a clan elder himself.
"When they shot Law in Toa-khe four years ago
It was because he was under the salt gabelle,
Collected the salt tax, not because he was a Christian."

❂ ❂ ❂

"What happened when you were captured, Tan?" I said
To a man who sat silently through the discussion,
Forty-odd, with deep lines around the mouth.
"I didn't have the luck that some of you had.
The Communists captured me and two of my daughters
And carried us away one rainy night.
The little one was only two years old,
And what with being scared and wet and worn out
She died the first week we spent up there in the mountains.
It was cold up there. There were forty or fifty of us
And our only shelter was overhanging rocks.
We sat, the women on one side, the men on the other,
Hands tied, feet shackled, each to the rest in the row.
If one had to go to the toilet, the whole row went,
And when we came back they tested all our leg-irons.
And when we slept we all had to lie the same way.
They untied our hands twice a day to let us eat.
If you looked around, they banged you with a gun-butt—
'Trying to escape, hey?' So we just looked down at the ground.

"And the lice were bad. Our hands tied the way they were,
We could catch the ones on our legs or on our necks,
But we couldn't get at our bodies, just let the lice suck.
And our wrists and ankles got raw pretty soon from the bonds.

"If you happened to be where the rain poured off the rocks,
That was your hard luck. They couldn't move the rest to suit you.
It was hardest on the old people. They got dysentery,
And the ones who sat and slept next to them would complain
They were getting dirty, so they'd put the sick by themselves
And they'd get cold and wet, and in a few days they'd die.
"After our ransom was arranged and paid, they took us
And led us around and over mountain paths.
If we looked up at all they banged us on the head.

Then they let us go and said, 'You've escaped, understand?
Don't tell 'em you paid a ransom. We don't take ransoms.
We're Reds, not bandits.' "

"What did you pay?" asked someone.
He hesitated, paled a little, and whispered, "Four hundred,
And over a hundred for my daughter."

Another said,
"They captured three of my brothers last year, let one go
With a demand for eight thousand for the others.
We can't get in touch with them now, for the soldiers are out
And making things hot for them. Then two months ago
The *bandits* got another of my brothers."

"But the Communists hate the bandits," said the youngster.
"You know that farmer who served us tea today?
He's the last man of a family of bandits.
His father and one brother were killed by Nanking troops,
One brother died of pneumonia, but the other four
Were caught in a cave and killed to a man by the Reds."

"The Reds and the Whites both shoot the Blacks," said another.
"The Blacks make believe they're Reds to scare the people.
The Reds say it's the Blacks who give them a bad reputation:
'Reds don't take ransoms—we carry on the class struggle.' "

"And the brother that's left?" I asked.

"He's safe if he behaves,
Tends his fields, and doesn't meddle in things."

"Yes,"
Said the youngster, "but in the two months since New Year's
The Whites have caught and shot a hundred people

Just between here and Changpu, and if you ask me,
About one bad one among them. The rest did nothing
But sell their rice to the Reds when they couldn't refuse.
Now the Whites are back in force and shoot them for it.
The people are out of luck whatever they do."

"And the people," I asked, "what do they think of the Reds?"

"Well, they're better than the Blacks, for they have *some* principles—
You know who *they* want to kill. They take us for ransom
To get the money to fight, but they're not like the bandits.
And the Reds are cleverer than the Whites, though
The Cantonese coming in now are pretty crafty.
Still, if the Whites ever chase the Reds out of here,
It'll be a happy day. They make too much trouble.
I wish they were ten thousand miles from here."

"Why don't they make peace with the Whites?" another asked.
"Chu and Naw have just joined the Nanking outfit—"

"Hah! I don't think this crowd are real Reds at all,"
Said one last. "They're just a clever bunch of bandits
Parading as Reds, the dirty hypocrites."

The thoughtful old man didn't agree with this:
"Well, I don't know. The Whites are uncovering stores
In caves in the mountains. Enough, they say, to support
Three hundred men for three years in a general revolt.
That doesn't sound like bandits. I think they'll join
Nanking now that the Reds up north have shown the way."

He was the clan elder, a member of the new chapel
We'd established two miles off. Three weeks later

The Reds came there disguised as Cantonese soldiers
Inspecting the place, seized the old man, and shot him.
His son escaped, but they entered and looted the house.

And five weeks later we heard that the same Red leader
Was suing for recognition by the government,
And that the Whites would probably take over his men.

And after the war when the Communists took power
They executed Pastor Tiu^{n} of Lam-sin.

Christmas Story

Said the pastor who'd been brought up on old Chinese stories:
"Kiang-goan went to the mountains to worship God,
But after she had prayed she stepped in God's footprint.
A violent trembling seized her and she conceived.
She gave birth to a boy, but, because he had no father,
She threw him out into a narrow alley
To be trodden to death by the cattle. But the cows
And goats knelt to him as they passed and suckled him.
She threw him on the ice. But from all directions
The birds flocked to him and covered and kept him warm.
She threw him out on a hillside. There the she-tigers
Suckled him, and a woodman found him there
And cared for him. The boy was Chiu Hok-tek,
Founder of his dynasty.

"So, too, our Lord
Came into the world, born without a human father.
But His birth was heralded by a choir of angels
And a great bright star in the east, and to Him came
Shepherds and wise men, humble and great, and brought
Their gifts to lay in reverence at His feet."

WAR

"No one tried to protect her. They gave her up."

Ground All Cleared

We came to a village where every house had been burned,
Although some ten or more had been rebuilt.
"My father and I once hid here from the bandits,"
The preacher said. "We used to have relatives here,
But they were killed by the Whites because they were Communists."

"That doesn't sound right," I said.

"It's right," he said.
"The Reds occupied this place about ten years ago
And stayed here about three years. Some of our Christians
Were ignorant people and let the Reds deceive them.
The Reds said that all should be share and share alike
Among rich and poor, no interest paid on money,
No rents on fields. Our people thought, 'Here are men
Who love the poor man. This is like the Gospel,
This is like Jesus' teaching.' So they joined them.
And then the Reds took them out to fight the Whites.

"Ai-yah! The Whites came in a couple of times
And shot all the men they could catch and burned some houses,
And when the Whites left the Reds came back again
And burned every house and shot almost every man.
The Reds said they had to tear down before they could build,
But all they ever had time for was tearing down,
And what they didn't tear down the Whites tore down."

A Call on the Fox

"Let's go over to see the commander," they said.
So we went out that Sunday afternoon,
The preacher who was our host in the little chapel,

The visiting Chinese pastor, and myself,
To see Keh, the man who ruled that mountain area.

A guard led us through the gate into the courtyard
Where the officers sat at a table playing mah jongg.
The commander had his bodyguard behind him
And a little automatic in his holster.
The orderly spoke to him; he snorted, smiled,
And rose to greet us ceremoniously.
He led us to his room. A guard stood at the doorway.
He bowed us to seats of honor. His cruel face relaxed.
In his hard eyes was a glint of good-natured laughter.

After the introductions, the pastor spoke:
"I met you once before when I was here
And reproached myself that I didn't speak to you then
About becoming a Christian. A man of your importance
In this district, a man of influence, a power for good,
Think what you could do if you gave yourself to Christ . . ."
Forthwith he gave a summary of the Gospels.

"That's bearding the bandit in his den," I thought.

The local man chimed in, "You're a good man,
You're famous far and wide for the good you do,
But if you want to be perfect—just join the church."

The commander heard them out blandly. His eyes twinkled
As he smiled and said in gentle deprecation,
"I'm ashamed. The trouble is that in my work
I have to go back and forth and around so much,
I'm afraid my attendance at church would be very irregular."

Tea was brought. The commander changed the subject.
The government had been annoying him of late.
"What can the government do in a place like this?

Their troops don't know the language, don't know the country.
A thousand bandits could hide here; *they'd* never find them.
There's never a bandit around when I'm in charge,
But only when troops come in and stir things up."
His lips compressed bitterly.

We took our leave,
Smiling and bowing. The pastor said in parting,
"I'm glad I saw you and had this chance to witness.
I hope that you will soon become a Christian."

He smiled. "I mean to. But, you see, I'm so busy."

Why We Forgot

He gave me thirteen hundred-dollar bills.
"These bills have 'Chungking' printed on them," he said,
"And I'm afraid there might be some question about them
If I try to use them here on Kulangsu,
For Chungking means Chiang Kai-shek, and the Japanese
Have set up Wang Ching-wei in Nanking and recognized him.
I thought if you took them up-country and used them up there
And gave me credit down here, it would be better."
Our treasurer was standing there beside him.
"Our friend here takes the risk of confiscation
When you go through inspection," he said. "You let me know
If the money goes through and what account it's in
And then I'll pay him." Our two Mission launches
Went from Kulangsu, the International Settlement,
Through the Japanese lines to Free China on the mainland.
One launch went to Seng-su, the other up the river
To Changchow.

I put the bills in my wallet. Inspection
Was mostly a matter of form, and anyway
I had never heard of any restriction on banknotes.
And there was no trouble. When I got to Changchow,
Because I was going to some meetings in Poa^{n}-a,
I gave the bills to Uncle John, and told him
The circumstances. He put them in the safe.

Then several things happened. The Japanese stopped all the launches.
Uncle John had taken the launch down to Kulangsu
And he was stuck there with all of his things up-country.
I couldn't get down to be with my family.
Then the Japanese bombed Talmage College again. We wondered,
Why? It never does much good to wonder.

After the meetings in Poa^{n}-a were over,
I had to go to some meetings in Hoa-an,
And on Monday, December 9th, I started walking
To Phaw-chui-khau to catch the boat to Sin-hi.
I caught a smaller boat loaded with baskets
Of duck eggs which were just hatching out. Two men
Went among the baskets continually, taking out shells
And making the baby ducks comfortable. Sometimes they put
An egg in a bowl of water to cool it; sometimes
They punched a hole in the shell with a thumbnail, and then
Put in a little water.

Our second day
They were towing us up Big Rapids at dusk.
They used a long woven-bamboo tow cable
And the towmen were on a hill on the far bank.
The tow cable caught on a rock and the boat began tipping.
The polers shouted and screamed at the men on the tow-path,
But they were too far away, and it was so dark
They couldn't see what was happening. They didn't slacken.

We had tipped 'way up. The boatman took an axe
And cut the cable. Zoom! We went down Big Rapids
Backward, amid much frenzied shouting and poling.

We tied up at a quiet spot by the bank,
And then began to call for the men to come.
They were on the other side of the river
And had to find the right spot to cross. We shouted
For about two hours before the men got back.

Next day we arrived in Sin-hi. A minor official
Was there and said Pearl Harbor had been bombed
By the Japanese on Monday morning (our time).
I wouldn't believe him, but he maintained it was so.
They were all glad the United States was in—
"Never mind," he said, "we'll kill them off together,"
And made a chopping motion with his hand.
I walked over the pass to Hoa-an that night
And Bill confirmed the news. His family
Was down in Kulangsu, too.

We listened to Don Bell
Broadcast from Manila. We heard the discussion
About blackout or no blackout, heard Manila proclaimed
An open city. I was attending a preachers' conference
In Hoa-an. I came home one afternoon
And we heard that the *Prince of Wales* and the *Repulse* were sunk.
We felt sunk, too. I didn't see my family
For four-and-a-half years.

Well, six or more months later,
A card from the treasurer came through the Japanese lines
Asking about the thirteen hundred dollars.
"Why does he write to me?" I asked Bill. "Uncle John
Is down there, living snug in the same house with him.
Why doesn't he ask him? I gave *him* the bills."

Evidently he wrote to me without inquiring,
And Uncle John had forgotten about it,
And I had dismissed the whole thing from my mind.

There was mail service across the lines. A certain proportion
Of letters got through. I wrote to the treasurer.

Months later a Chinese pastor came
With written authorization from the man
Who gave me the money, to collect the bills from me.
I investigated. The bills were still in the safe,
In a separate envelope. Uncle John,
Because he had to take the launch right down,
Had intended to make the entry when he came back.

I apologized; "A dollar is only a dime"
Was the current word. The original bills
Were worth about one-tenth their former value.

Like Water

We wanted to have a prayer meeting in the house
And no one could find the Bible. The pastor said,
"You're all Christians here. Why don't you have prayers
And learn to read the hymn-book and the Bible?
The only ones who can read here are the women
Who learned the Romanized in the Woman's School."

"You wouldn't have household prayers either," said a woman,
"If you had to go out and sleep in the woods all night."

"Why?" I asked. "Are the bandits running again?"

"No," she said, "the government wants to arrest them
And make them all go into the army. The head of the ward
Sent word that two of our men will have to go.

The other day they came with a couple of soldiers
And said they wanted to talk to us about taxes,
But that was just a blind. When we met with them,
They arrested one of our boys and took him away.
They shouldn't have done it. He is far too young for the draft."

"Haven't you any men who are of draft age?"

"Yes,
They were all in the woods. They took the youngster
To hold as hostage."

Said another woman,
"The head of the ward says two must go, and now
We're always fighting. Each family wants the other
To give up a son and be done with it."

"That's the trouble,"
The pastor said, "you folks are all so ignorant.
Why don't you go and see the head of the ward,
Find out what he wants, and make some arrangement with him.
The draft is a government thing. It's everywhere.
It's just because we're fighting a war. Just go to him
And tell him you're willing to make a fair arrangement.
You can't keep on like this."

Then one of the men,
A fellow in his twenties, began to cry.
"We can't trust him," he sobbed. "If we didn't hide,
He'd take us all. Other folks get their sons off
Because they have money or influence. We haven't any."

The pastor turned to me and heaved a sigh.
"There's something in that," he said. "Here in China
The heaviest burdens are borne by the poorest people.
The government requisitions are like water;
They find the lowest level."

Death of the Fox

The Tiger, the Bull, and the Fox were killed. Those years
After Pearl Harbor were the most peaceful I've known
In South Fukien. We never thought of bandits,
But traveled anywhere, anytime, day or night.

The Bull was taken first. He didn't think
They had anything against him; he was willing
To cooperate in the war effort within reason.
He was the best of the bandits. He was better
Than most of the officials or generals, but he was down
As a bandit, and when they took him they had a list
Of his offenses as long as your arm. It was true
He'd killed plenty of soldiers when they were after him.
And he'd disregarded orders from above
When they didn't suit him, but in that he was usually right.
He also was taken to Foochow and shot. Afterward
They dug up all the silver he had buried.
When the government called in silver, he'd called it in too—
And buried it.

The Fox was a different type;
He couldn't be lured. He could deceive the officials.
They couldn't fool him. He would say the right things,
But they couldn't get him to leave the An-khoe hills.
They had never been able to catch him there, but this time
They had a good man on the job. He marched in his troops
Through An-khoe this way, that way, always
Going somewhere else. The outside circle
Was drawn before the Fox discovered his plan.
Then he began to draw the inside circle,
To squeeze the Fox. The villagers didn't dare
To give him information. They feared the Fox.
He would call in all the ward leaders and promise protection.

They had heard that promise too many times before,
They wouldn't believe it. Then he would say to them,
"All right, I'll have to move you. Tell me tonight
Which men are bandits and where they are, or tomorrow
I'm going to drive the whole village out of this area."
Then they believed he meant business, and told what they knew.

The Fox couldn't break the cordon. Each time he tried
He lost some men. The soldiers came closer and closer.
The Fox was on the run then. But it was strange:
Almost all of his men were taken or killed,
His lieutenants and relatives were shot down at his side,
But he always escaped.

He had arranged for a raft
To take him and a few men across to Chiang-peng County,
And was working his way to the raft when he was wounded.
He told his brother-in-law to leave him and run for it
With the men who remained. But he stayed, and they fought
Until they were exterminated. That was once
That the government did exterminate bandits. They beheaded
The Fox and sent his head to all the towns
In the county, so people could know he was really dead.

Said a man to me afterward, "We have no bandits.
All the others were killed, killed down to the last man
Before they got Keh. There's no one able
To start things up again; the worst we have now
Are the smallest of small thieves." I saw the Fox's new home,
Burned now and ruined. I asked them, "Why do that?
If you get the man, you needn't burn the house."

They said, "No one ever caught Keh before."

Death of the Tiger

The Tiger had weathered many emergencies. The government
Would often announce that soldiers had been dispatched
To exterminate him. He would always withdraw
To the hills around Lam-khi^n and Tsun-tiu^n;
And each time the government came to terms with him.
The war was his undoing. He was offered
A command if he would fight the Japanese,
And he accepted. The next step was to get him
Away from his home grounds. He and his soldiers
Were sent to Foochow. He was given assurance
That he would command a brigade on the Chekiang front.
They arrested him in Foochow and shot him.

His wife
Was a member of our Sio-khe church. The pastor
Called on her regularly, and when I was home
I accompanied him. Sometimes the Tiger was there.
And then the pastor would preach the Gospel to him,
And he would nod as the pastor made his points
And say Christianity was good. It taught people to be good.
He may well have believed that, because his wife
And his daughter-in-law were very fine women. The girl
Was a graduate of the kindergarten school
Run by the English Presbyterians on Kulangsu.
His son had been killed in an earlier attempt to exterminate him.
After the Tiger was executed, the government
Allowed these women to inherit some of his property.

But his concubine in Lam-khi^n met a violent death.
She acted for the Tiger when he was away
And, though a young woman, she was quite as heartless
As he ever was, and everyone hated her.
After the Tiger was killed, the villagers

Went to the Tiger's headquarters and asked for her.
No one tried to protect her. They gave her up,
And the villagers took her down to the river and drowned her.

Lotus

We had two churches in town. Rose, the Bible woman,
Was employed by the Mission, not assigned to work
In either church, but assigned to the country churches.
She was, however, a member of the First Church,
Was elected deacon there, then elder. When she was home,
She attended church there, and consistory meeting,
And went calling with the other consistory members.

The pastor of the Second Church, an ambitious man,
Felt bitter about this. He would often reproach her
For giving all her attention to one church,
But Rose would insist, "I'm not working for them,
My work is in the country. All I do,
I do as a member and officer of that church."
This didn't satisfy him.

Rose was a widow,
And had a son, an only son, in Singapore.
Before he went overseas, his mother arranged
His betrothal to Lotus, a girl in Second Church,
A niece to one of the elders. War came. And more war.
The Japanese took Singapore. Communication
Became more and more difficult. For over six months
Rose had no letters from her son. The pastor
Of Second Church, out of dissatisfaction with Rose,
Would say to Lotus, "He'll never marry you.
He's married someone else down south. Else why
Haven't you heard for so long?"

"The war," she said.

"Other people get letters," he answered, "you know that.
If he kept on writing, you'd surely get a few letters."

Lotus went to Rose and said to her,
"He keeps talking to me like that every time he sees me.
I don't believe what he says, but it makes me feel sad.
And now he has my relatives talking that way."

Said Rose, "I'm sorry. From what I know of my son,
I don't believe it either. But how can we prove it?
So far as I am concerned, though you have not married
I always look upon you as the wife of my son,
And I am happy to think of you in that way.
If, however, you or your family wish,
Because of this separation, to break the engagement,
I wouldn't oppose you. I would respect your wish."

"I don't want to break it," replied the girl.
"I feel more at one with you than I do with my family.
But it's hard, when I live over there, to have the pastor
Throw it up to me day after day."

"In that case," said Rose,
"Why don't you go off to school? Take a two-year course
In the Woman's School. It will interest you,
And if this war keeps on you can find some work
In the church as a Bible woman."

She went to school,
Got into new surroundings, enjoyed herself.
There was only one thing wrong. No letters came.
It seemed as if everyone heard from overseas
Except her. And every time she came home for vacation,
The pastor and her family harped on the same old subject:

Her fiancé must have married someone else.

Lotus finished a year and a half of school,
Came home for a spring vacation. First Church asked her
To lead a prayer meeting. A day or two later,
One of the elders approached her, said the consistory
Would like to call her to be their Bible woman
After she graduated. She was pleased and excited
And said she'd be glad to accept if they really wanted her.

When the pastor of Second Church heard it, he was furious.
"Why did you accept?" he asked Lotus

She replied,
"They asked me. They were the only ones who asked me."
"We took it for granted you'd come to us," he said.
"Don't you belong to our church? We didn't ask you
Because you still have a term in school. I know,
It was all arranged by that pseudo-mother-in-law.
She not only ties you up with her worthless son,
But she takes you away from your church." He kept it up
And had the girl in tears. Then, day after day,
Throughout the vacation, he would scold her and scorn her.

Lotus would visit Rose and find comfort there,
But that would provoke the pastor still more. At last
Time came to return to school and she set out.
It was a two-day walk. For most of the first day,
The road ran along the shore, and then it turned inland.
No news came for a week. Then word came
That a young girl's body had been found in a cove near a village
Twenty miles away, at a place where the road left the shore.

Rose and some of Lotus' family went there.
They had buried Lotus the morning after they found her,
But they showed her Bible and a little cloth bundle

She had left at the turn of the road. So they knew it was she,
And decided to leave the body where it was.
One man said he had seen her sitting there
At the turn of the road, first reading a book she had,
Then wringing her hands and sobbing. A little later
He looked again and she was gone. A woman
Told how an old man had sat with the body.
"She must have been a good person," she said, "or otherwise
How would she have such good fortune? This old man
Wanted to do a good deed before he died
And volunteered to watch the body all night
Until we could bury it. It's seldom a stranger
Is cared for and buried as she was here. She was lucky."

It was suicide. Rose remembered that recently
Someone had mentioned a body discovered somewhere,
And Lotus had said, "They'll never find my body,"
But Rose thought she'd misunderstood, and dismissed the remark.

Thunderstruck

"The end of last month," said Bess, "just after supper,
It was Sunday, May 31st, the end of the month,
We saw in the west a terrific thunderstorm coming.
And just then the warning sounded. We thought, 'What now?
What plane would be flying with this fearful storm coming on?'
The lightning kept flashing, the thunder rolled and crashed.
We had to shout to each other in order to hear.
Then the rain came down. For twenty minutes
It came down in torrents. In ten minutes more it was over.

"Next day I went to the church, and there on the sidewalk
I saw a great heap of wood, beams and broken boards,

Old and weathered and splintered—like the remains
Of a broken house. And that is what they were.

"I thought some place had been bombed the night before,
But they said the warning had only been for practice.
They practice on the last night of every month.
The house had been struck by lightning. The people had gone
To the church to live with the pastor, and had brought
Some wood from the house along for fuel. A widow
With five small children, and one other woman, a guest,
Had been in the house.

"On Tuesday afternoon
At the prayer meeting the widow recounted the story.
'The thunder was rolling, the rain was pouring down.
I was just putting things away in a table drawer
When I happened to glance at the roof and saw the sky.
I quickly hid under the table, and down came the roof!
Praise the Lord! We were under His protecting care.
What a marvelous deliverance. All of the children
Were safe, and even the chickens and ducks. Our goose
We found buried up to the neck, but when we freed her
She walked about as if nothing had happened. Our guest
Was in the front room upstairs, and she was struck.
Was killed, but that was a judgment: She was bad.'

" 'How do you know she was bad?' I asked her later.
'A thunderbolt never hits a pregnant woman
Unless she's done something bad,' she said. 'When her husband
Heard she'd been thunderstruck, he wouldn't come to look;
He wouldn't make arrangements for her burial.' "

Anatomy Lesson

In the summer of nineteen forty-three,
We had our general youth conference on the campus
Of Talmage College. Things went along smoothly except
For a flood in the city which made it difficult
For outside speakers to get to us. Sirens sounded
Once in a while, but no planes ever came
Until the next-to-last day, just before we began
The afternoon session. Then we saw three planes
Headed straight for us. We quickly got out of sight.
Some stood under trees. Some went into the caves
The Communists had dug there in 'thirty-two
When they were afraid the Nationalists would bomb them.
Another group, I among them, went down a hill
Off the campus's west side to a sunken pathway
Between a field and a little bamboo grove.

On the way down we passed some crumbling mounds,
Graves of deserters who had been executed
In the days of Tiu^{n} Ge. From one of these mounds
A skull jarred loose, rolled across our path
In front of one of the boys. "Oooo-oooh!" he said,
And shuddered. We all kept moving. The planes
Flew low, so low we could see the men in them, but they passed on.

The all-clear sounded. "Funny they didn't bomb,"
Said someone. "The city is flooded, foundations and walls
Are water-logged. A bomb dropped anywhere
Would bring down the houses around it and kill the people."

We came to the skull. One student, I remember,
Had wooden clogs on his feet. He put one clog
On the skull and rolled it gently back and forth.
The science teacher was with us. The student pointed

To the sutures and said, "Is that the way a skull
Is divided?" And the teacher took a few minutes
To explain to them the structure of the skull.

Good Friday

When horror crushes flesh and bone and marrow,
When death through playing children drives its furrow,
When mothers stumble stupefied with sorrow,

Then I study
Thy broken body.

When lie and callous lust become the fashion,
When cruelty comes surging in like ocean,
When in my heart as well hate would take station,

Then I find good
Thy poured-out blood.

The Shooting

At the close of evening prayers in the doctor's shop—
Shots. Our host jumped to close and bar the door
As a crowd of people, feet pounding, fled past.
Then quiet.

"It's nothing," said one of the men in the shop.
"It's when they keep on shooting that something's doing.
Why, when I was in Changchow at the West Gate there
In '32, we'd be scared half out of our wits
Whenever we heard some shooting. We ran five times
From the West Gate down to the Circle, and all for nothing.
When the Reds did come you can bet that everyone knew it.

We had never heard any shooting like that before;
The real thing had come at last."

The preacher had gone.
He came back in a moment. "A man was shot in the street.
A soldier. He ran out of headquarters and they killed him."

As the preacher and I walked home, a good-looking young man
From headquarters joined us. "I hope you weren't alarmed.
A man behaved badly and we had to get rid of him.
Good night."

"Good night." We went quietly home in the dark.

After He Had Sung a Hymn

One day a Chinese pastor and I went to visit
The chapel at An-jin. Because of bandit troubles,
No one had visited it for about twelve years.
But a deal was made with the bandits during the war
And the road was opened again.

Inside the church
The villagers had stored rice baskets and mats,
Wooden rakes and tools, and a fanning mill.
There was no one around, but from a nearby house
A woman was watching us, and she called to us.
Her husband, Lau, was the only church member left,
And he, herself, and their son the only Christians.
She gave us a drink made out of some kind of leaves,
A substitute for tea, and asked us to stay
Until the men came home from the fields.

We stayed
And talked and had prayers with the family after supper.

None of them could read, but Lau knew how to pray.
Then I made my bed on some boards laid across two benches
And the pastor went to sleep with the son in the loft.
Lau was so happy we had come to see him
That he walked six miles with us the following morning,
Talking and asking questions, taking his leave
When we came to the main road again.

After that,
Whenever I made that circuit, about twice a year,
I used to visit them. But then, one time,
About three years after we had first gone to see them,
The woman said Lau had died three months before.
"When he knew he was going to die," she said, "he called us
And told us we must be faithful to the doctrine
Because it was the true doctrine about the one God.
And he told the boy to be sure to remember that.
Then he sang a hymn," (she didn't know which one)
"And said he was going to Heaven. And he passed."
She showed us an unmarked grave on a slope near the house.

INFLATION

"How much will you give me if I save you?"

Prodigal

Said the Bible woman, ". . . And when the younger son
Got to the far country, what did he do? Did he think
Of his father's home? No, he thought only of himself.
He wasted his substance in riotous living. A lot
Of fair-weather friends came in to help him spend his money,
And spent it all. Then—a famine. How stupid of him.
We know that a time of famine or other trouble
Is when a clever man can make lots of money,
But he had wasted his money and had to herd pigs.
And he ate worse than the pigs. He envied them.

"Why didn't he do as Joseph did? Joseph
Also went to a far country, sold as a slave.
But he was clever, explained the Emperor's dream,
And the Emperor made him prime minister. There, too,
They had a famine, and look what Joseph did.
He got all the land for the Emperor, and he himself
Became a rich man. And he didn't forget his father.
He was able to give his father plenty of grain
And many rich presents, and also showed his father
How to get pasture rights in the land of Goshen."

Distance

The preacher said, "Loa's married her to a heathen,
But he's son of the big clan elder, so Loa gets protection.
They were glad to get her because she's so good looking,
And young and used to good hard work as well.
I told Loa not to. They won't let her come to church.
They despise the church! Our members are all nobodies.
But they wanted the girl and were willing to pay a good price.

Loa was afraid to refuse them—and wanted the money.
I thought we could marry her to a Christian in Leng-soa^{n},
A fine young fellow, but Loa said that was too far,
Like saying Goodbye to his daughter forever.

"—*Maybe!*
But which is farther, Leng-soa^{n} or Hell, is what *I* say."

Measure for Measure

"I *thought* I wasn't getting enough rice," said Liu
"And now I find the deacon's been cheating me
For over a year. I didn't know there was a difference
Between the local measure and standard measure.
The local measure is smaller. He measured the rice
Out to me by local measure, but in the accounts
He put down standard measure. It made a difference
Of about two catties on every measure I got."

"Did he put it in his own pocket?" I asked?

"It seems not,"
Said Liu. "Contributions were made in rice
And the rice is still there. He thinks that's the way to do business.
If I'm too stupid to ask what he means by a measure,
Then he would be foolish not to seize that advantage.
He seems to be trying, as deacon, to act for the church
As he would act for himself."

"What about the others?"
I asked. "Did they know about it?"

"His father did.
He's an elder. He thought his son was pretty clever.
The others hadn't known he was doing this,

But they weren't surprised, considering I was so innocent.
He'd only done what most of them would have done."

Profit for God

"When we have to make a decision," he said, "we must ask,
'If I do this, am I making a profit for God?'
Many times there is the chance of profit for me,
But God is the loser. Then again it may turn out
That I must lose to make a profit for God.

"You see before you a threadbare evangelist
Who has wandered down from Hopeh, preaching the Gospel
From city to city and from town to town.
Wherever the Lord calls me, there I go.
My wife and child travel with me, share my lot,
Good fortune and ill, gratitude and neglect.
For I have no fixed income. God touches the hearts
Of those to whom I minister. Like the apostle,
'I know how to be abased and how to abound.'

"Yet back in Hopeh I was a rich man's son.
Now that paper money is no good, it is the fashion
To wear gold rings. I used to wear gold rings,
A ring on every finger. No tenth-of-an-ounce ones,
But each one a full half-ounce, pure yellow gold.
I ate rich food every day. I wore a silk gown,
A jacket of black brocade, and leather shoes.
You may think I had a good life. I lived in Hell.

"There was my father, and there were five of us brothers,
All dissolute, headstrong, quarrelsome, always fighting.
Almost every night we drank and gambled and fought.
My father would get drunk and scream at my brothers

And they would fight with him until the servants
Pulled them away and helped them to their rooms.

"I was the youngest. One night I ran away.
I became a soldier. I joined Feng Yu-hsiang's army,
You remember him. The Christian general.
He was fair with me. He kept good discipline
And gave us enough to eat. We had prayers every day
And Bible reading, and Christian evangelists there,
And I was baptized along with a lot of others.
But I wasn't converted then. It was just a form.

"Later, when we were fighting another general,
I was one of the guards at a mountain pass.
It was lonely up there, and cold, and I thought to myself,
'Why am I here? What am I doing this for? Why don't
I get out of this?' But there wasn't anything else
I wanted to do.

"Then I met another man
In our unit, a real Christian, and he taught me
How to pray, how to interpret the Bible, how to commune
With God to learn His will for me. God called me
Then to be an evangelist, and I left
The army and went wherever the Spirit led.
From the north I sojourned to Shanghai, to Foochow,
To Chuanchow, and now here. I have no thought
If the place to which I am led is large or small,
The people few or many, rich or poor.
I want to do what God would have me do
And my endeavor in every situation
Is to make a profit for God.

"On the boat coming here,
I had been misinformed about the fare

And didn't have enough money, but I had
A gold ring which had been given me in Chuanchow,
So I told the captain I would cash the ring.
He acted displeased, and offered the Changchow rate.
Now everybody knows that Chuanchow gold is better,
That Changchow gold has more base alloy added,
And I could have argued the point. I was bigger than he was
And I wasn't afraid of him. But I thought to myself,
'If you start a row, you may get the right price for your ring,
And that will be profit, but will it be profit for God?'
So I acquiesced, and said, 'All right, take it. Take it.'

"After we got to the church, my wife went out shopping.
She came back and said, 'I changed a hundred dollars,
And the man in the shop gave me a hundred coppers.'
'A hundred coppers,' I said, 'that's a good exchange!'
(I hadn't been here long.) I said, 'Tell me the shop,
I'll go and exchange some more.' So I went there,
But the man said, 'No, I can't exchange your money.
I made a mistake with your wife. I gave her a hundred
Instead of ten coppers, and now you come to me
And expect me to do it again.' I could have gotten angry.
I could have walked away. My wife had the coppers.
I said, 'My friend, I have just arrived in this town.
I know nothing about your exchange rates. If you, by mistake,
Gave my wife a hundred coppers instead of ten,
I owe you ninety coppers, and I shall repay them.'
His heart softened. We became friends. It was profit for God."

Rescue

The An-hai launch capsized. Some bandits aboard
Murdered a man. As soon as the shooting started,
The passengers all rushed to the opposite rail
And the loaded boat went over. It was near shore
And many small boats put out to rescue the people,
But not indiscriminately. They bargained with them—
"How much will you give me if I save you?"

Some agreed to anything and climbed into a boat.
Others backed off and looked for another rescuer.
And others gave up and drowned; the price was too high.

The Three Trees

Whenever I visit Law-khe in Ping-ho County
And walk along the road between Tham-phoe
And Hong-thau-poa^{n}, I like to watch the river
Play at acrobatics in the gorge below.
Especially at a place where three pine trees
Mark a path to a small ravine to the right. I often
Pause a minute or two to see the water
First somersault in white foam over rocks
Then slip demurely deep green into pools.
It has a cooling, restful effect on me.

The path to the right leads up past a few farmhouses
To a big, square house with a courtyard in the middle,
The house of the Gaw family, one of the first
Two families in the area to become Christian.
Before the father died, I often went there
And spent the night, and sometime the next morning
They would call everyone in, and I would hold

A communion service. I would stay for lunch
And after lunch would walk to Hong-thau-poa^{n}.

After the father died, I went there more seldom
For the younger folk were able to walk to church.
The eldest son served as deacon for several years
And then was elected elder, a taciturn fellow,
Forty-five years old.

About six months
After the election, I came again to the church
To install the new officers. I asked for Gaw.
The men looked at each other. "Gaw's not home."

"Then we'll have to postpone his installation
Until I come again," I said.

They answered,
"We don't think we ought to install him. He's in jail."

"What did he do?" I asked.

"He sold stolen goods."
"What did he have to sell stolen goods for?" I asked.
"He has plenty of money."

"Not anymore,"
They answered. "He speculated and went broke.
Paper money was depreciating fast,
And he borrowed a hundred thousand at ten percent.
Ten percent a *month,* and bought water buffaloes.
He held the buffaloes, but then sold at a loss
Because his creditors came after him.
He was supposed to pay interest every month,
And he had to sell his own buffaloes besides
In order to pay the interest.

"At that time,
There was a rascal in the farmhouse below Gaw
Who was head of a gang that was stealing buffaloes.
Because Gaw's house had an inside court, this fellow
Asked Gaw to let him sleep in one of the rooms
And keep the stolen cattle in the courtyard.
Gaw knew the cattle were stolen; his brothers didn't.
They thought he was buying them. Gaw was persuaded
To sell the stolen cattle for a commission.
People became suspicious. Soldiers came
And there was a battle at the farmhouse below,
But the thieves stood the soldiers off. Then we had rain,
A flood. The thieves escaped. Gaw's relatives,
His uncle, his brothers, his cousins, and their families,
All moved out. Then the soldiers came back and burned
The farmhouse below and half of Gaw's house, and Gaw
Was caught and put in jail."

"I'm sorry to hear
All this about Gaw," I said.

"There's other news,"
They said. "Gaw's sister-in-law was drowned in the flood.
A good woman, she was the daughter of Lim, the deacon.
When she heard the shooting and learned what was going on
And that Gaw was implicated, she wouldn't wait
For her husband to come home, but started right in
To move their stuff out. She shouldered the burdens herself,
And carried the things to some friends half a mile away.
Then it began to rain hard and they tried to get her
To stop, but she wouldn't stop. She was weeping and angry
And said she wouldn't live one day more in a house
With thieves and bandits. When the floods began,

She had to cross that little brook up there,
But by the time she got to it with her load
It was raging among the boulders. A couple of men
Were standing there, afraid to go through the water;
Though it was only six feet from side to side,
The gully was three feet deep. They tried to stop her,
But she was obsessed and walked into the torrent. In one spit,
She was swept off down the ravine and battered naked
On the great boulders standing there. They found her body
Floating at the bend in the river just below town,
With trees and lumber from bridges and wrecked houses."

I murmured sympathy. One of the men said then,
"It was sad, pastor. But, you know, right after that
Something funny happened that made the whole village laugh.
It was market day. Someone went to a young man
Who lived up the river and said, 'They've found the body
Of a young woman. It looks like your wife.'
He ran down to the river bank, took one glance,
And cried out, 'It is! It is!' He sat down on the sand,
Took up the body, embraced it, and wept aloud.
After a while he went back to the market
To arrange for the body's removal. But Lim, the deacon,
Had also been told. He recognized his daughter
And had the body taken to his home.

"When the young man came back, the body was gone. He was frantic.
He asked people where it had gone to. Then a friend asked,
'Are you sure that was your wife's body you saw?
I've just come from the village. Your wife was there
Safe and sound when I left.' Bewildered, he went home.
It was true. His wife was sitting outside the front door,
Suckling the baby. She'd already heard the news
And scolded him for making a fool of himself.

And everybody teased him about it."

Some months later
When I came again, I asked what had happened to Gaw.
"His brothers," they said, "were able to raise enough money
To get him out of jail. The other man,
The leader of the thieves, had killed a man.
His case was harder to settle. But he had money,
Silver dollars hidden away, and he was able
To buy his way back here again, even though
The relatives of the man he had killed had been trying
For months to get the government to take action.
But they were poor villagers. They had no influence.

"So he came back, went to market bold as you please,
Stood around, talked to people to show he wasn't afraid;
He could buy the officials off. But he might have known
The murdered man's relatives would be unsatisfied
To see him get off scot-free. Along toward dusk
He started home. You remember the three pine trees?
He took the path there and he was ambushed and killed."

All Smoothed Over

They brought an official into the Mission hospital,
The head of the county's department of education.
The man had typhoid. The Chinese doctor in charge
Received him, gave him a private room. They wanted
A special nurse, but there were only two nurses.
As it was, they gave a great deal of time to the man
For he was very ill and sometimes delirious.
Men from his office often came to see him
And asked the doctor to do this or that for him.

One night, in delirium, the man got out of bed.
They put him back and watched him, but next day he died.

Alleging malpractice, some ten or more men from his office
Came to punish the doctor. The doctor ran.
They fired at him, caught him, knocked him down,
Kicked him and pummeled him with their gun-butts. Then
They went to the magistrate with a formal accusation
Of malpractice. When we brought the assault to his notice,
The magistrate sided against the doctor. The best
He could offer was that, if we preferred no charges,
He would see that the other side withdrew theirs.
We agreed. A lawsuit is too much like a war,
Easy to start, but no one knows where it will end.

"Those fellows are all from their chief's village," said a friend,
"And when he died they all lost their jobs. That's why
They were in such a rage."

The doctor was laid up
For a week or more. A month or two later,
When Synod met in town, the magistrate
Had a tea for us all, and told us he realized
The good work both missions and Church were doing in China.

Incident on the Road

I was going up the mountain from Hoe-khe
To Chhi-a-na, the little road to Leng-na,
When I heard panting and heavy footfalls behind me.
Three soldiers ran past me. After an interval
Two soldiers with guns ran past. A little further
Along the road I found three discarded knapsacks
Lying open and the rice spilled out on the stones.

Then I heard shots. I came to a place where the road
Makes a big curve around a steep ravine.

There I saw two soldiers, just youngsters, on their knees,
Guarded by one of the armed men. The other was looking
Down into the ravine. I kept walking toward them
And the man who was guarding the boys called out to me,
"It's all right, sir. Come on. Go right ahead.
I'm sorry if we've disturbed you. We're catching deserters."

I went on to Chhi-a-na. I was sitting inside the inn
When I saw the third boy go by. He didn't see me.
He was out of breath and his uniform was disordered
From running through brush. He spoke a few hurried words
To the innkeeper and went on. The innkeeper came inside.
He looked at me and looked puzzled. Then he asked,
"Did you see or hear of bandits along the road?"

"No," I said.

Advance Rumors

"They tell me beef is cheaper," I said to the cook.
"They're killing more buffaloes," she said. "There's a rumor
That the Reds will arrest a man with more than one,
And they're killing the extra ones. And cloth has gone up.
The rumor is, people mustn't wear good clothes,
So they're getting suits of that coarse gray stuff, like the Communists."

"But the Communists aren't here yet. We don't know
What they'll do. That talk may not be true at all."

"Folks are afraid. They think it's smart to seem poor."

A Warning

The pastor and I were out preaching to a village.
He had me speak first; then he got up to speak.
"You see this man who has spoken? He's an American.
See how much taller he is than the rest of us?
That's because they worship God in America.
In the days of Sung we Chinese were ten feet tall
And we lived a hundred years. But we worshipped idols,
And as we worshipped idols our bodies got smaller,
And our lives grew shorter until we are where we are now.
In America their lives are becoming longer,
Their bodies larger and stronger. They worship God.
And we must worship God if we want to grow;
If we keep on worshiping idols, we'll dwindle to nothing!"

A Caution

"The pastor had a naturally resonant voice,"
Said Nelson, "and wasn't too careful of what he said;
He never worried much about what people thought.
He was sitting in our living room in Changchow
Saying things which few at that time dared to utter,
Confident that I would understand him—
When in came our cook with the tea-tray. He liked the pastor,
And was moved to tell us something we did not suspect.
" 'Every day when I go to the market,' he said, 'I stop
At police headquarters and report, and they question me
About who was here and what they were doing here.
I'm forced to do this. I'm just telling you.'

"The pastor's face went white. We drank our tea
In silence, and he said a subdued goodbye."

Bible Woman's Report

The Bible woman had spent some months in a village
Two miles from the nearest church. She had worked with the women,
Trying to teach them to read the Romanized,
And had held a little prayer meeting every night.
The boys were a rowdy lot and used to tease her.

"When I first got there," she said, "they gave me a room
That was half full of brush and bracken stored for fuel.
I wanted it out, but they said, 'What harm does it do?'
And I had to carry the whole of it out myself.
Below the room where we used to have our meetings
Was the room where they had the idol, and after dusk
The men would sit there and talk. And people would come
And ask the idol what medicine to use.
Or if they'd get well again, or if the baby
Was going to be a boy. And Christian men
Would sit and talk and laugh, and sometimes one
Would ask the idol a question. I didn't like it.
It wasn't good for them to be sitting there,
And I spoke to one of the older men about it.

"Then the boys decided to tease me, and one of the women
Said she heard one of them say that when we met
He was going to pelt me with cow dung through the window.
So I went and got his mother to come to the meeting
And had her sit right beside me, and he didn't dare.

But one day they put a big ant's nest in the doorway.
We didn't notice but went right on with the meeting
And soon we had big red ants over everything.

"So I went to see the clan elder. I didn't blame them,
But I spoke very carefully, said they were only teasing.
And when I left they all wanted me to stay longer."

Communists

". . . They made the meshes daily smaller."

Valley Landscape, Sin-kio

Down the burned-over hillside, down the old
Stone steps, down to peach and pear bloom, down to spring.

A lifeless, leaden purple are the leaves
Which cling to the liquid-amber; and the boughs
Of the pride-of-India, leafless, are still laden
With last year's berries, black and shriveled now.
Cane fields are stubble; leaves stripped from their stalks
A month ago lie on their plots in ashes.
The rice fields, silvery, dusty gray, await now
Mattock or plow. The mustard's at every season's end;
The ruffled leaves are hung in every yard
From clothes-pole, rack, and stand, are laid on the roof
Of hen-house, pig-pen, gateway, along with trays
Of thin-sliced mustard hearts, to be dried and salted,
Smeared with the lees of wine, and stored in jars.

Yet, it is spring. In scattered squares of green
Along the somber valley the spring crops glisten,
Dark green fields of wheat not yet in head,
Fields of peas in white and purple bloom,
And patches of oil-plant, pale green and spangled
With shining yellow flowers.

On the balks
And margins of the road are violets,
Azalea blooms, like lavender butterflies,
Flutter above the black, burned-over strips,
And other flowers, blue, red, yellow, white,
And white-drifted bushes, bearing bloom like snow
Helped redeem the waste of hill and wood.

And this is the season of peach and pear bloom; radiant
Peach and pear, their blossoms pink and white,

Star the untidy hillside. They frame and soften
The earthen walls of village homes and brighten
The brown-black water of the pool. Beyond,
On flooded fields, like peach-blossom concentrate,
Deeper, far deeper in shade, but like in tone,
Duckweed floats in a trembling flood of color.

Enthusiast

I first met Po when he was a student in Talmage.
He'd been fired by Sung's preaching, and was determined
To be another Sung. I heard him preach
And he *was* a Sung, down to the last detail,
Lacking only Sung's authority and power.

That phase must have passed. I had expected
To find him in Seminary after he graduated.
He married a preacher's daughter, but that was as near
As he ever got to the ministry. Instead
He became an executive in the Nationalist party,
Bustling about among his old friends, exhorting
Them to a more fervent patriotism. He lost
His interest in the Church, but he would accept
Invitations to preach. Then, usually, he took
A text from the Bible as springboard and gave the group
A talk exalting all that the Party had done,
Was doing, would do, and told what the Church
Should do to support the Party in its progress.

Then the Communists came. I hadn't heard of Po
Or thought of him for several years. A teacher
From our primary school went down to Changchow on a visit,
And when he returned asked me if I knew Po.
I said, "Yes, he was one of the little Sungs at Talmage."

He chuckled. "He's lost all his Christianity now.
He says they fooled him once with their talk about Christ,
But they won't again. He's in the Girls' Middle School
In Changchow, in the office. He's become
The leader of a group of teachers and students
Who want to eliminate all religious courses
And expel all foreign teachers from the school.
Everyone knows he's a Bible woman's son,
And a preacher's son-in-law, and a former secretary
Of the Nationalist party, but he confessed all that
A week ago and said he had seen the light."

The Student Mind

Dick heaved a sigh. "I wish my students would do
For others what I try to do for them.
They gave some talks on health last night in the church,
But you should have heard some of the jargon they employed.
They reeled off a string of passages from their textbooks
That made no sense whatever to simple laymen,
And most of the audience couldn't read even a newspaper.
They don't care what the people got out of their talks
So long as they show what *they* know. Someday, they hope,
They'll be able to turn that omniscience into something.

"But in the classroom—that's something else again.
They parrot the book. 'Yes, but what does that *mean*?'
Then they're stumped. But if *I* depart one jot from the book
In one of my lectures, they're after me full-cry.
And if I make an error, no matter what kind,
I can see their eyes gleam as one of them questions me
To bring it out." He grinned. "Those crazy kids."

An Exceeding Weight of Glory

How did the Reds keep track of everybody?
They couldn't at first, but we could see their grip
Tighten gradually. They organized
All kinds of associations: teachers, students,
Doctors, nurses, farmers, women—everyone
Belonged to at least one association, controlled
Through democratic centralism by the Party,
And guided by disciplined Party men in their midst.

They required everyone to commit himself—
Raise his fist and shout the slogans! March
In the parades, attend the demonstrations in the parks,
Serve on the committees, write the confessions of error.
They had their watchers to see if any hung back
(Mrs. Sim wouldn't raise her fist and shout the slogans),
Watching at meetings, watching in the parks.

They reduced mobility. Passes were required
For travel from one town to another. Guests
Had to be reported, and absences from home.
Squads knocked at the doors of selected houses each night,
Entered the inns and got the guests out of bed,
Requiring each to explain his presence there.

Taxes, levies, fund drives, charities, raids
Enabled them to study and classify everyone
Who had anything. Every teacher had his dossier,
And wrote under their guidance his autobiography.

They encouraged informers, encouraged men to denounce
Their friends and fellow workers, encouraged children
To denounce their fathers and mothers, aunts and uncles,
Encouraged students to denounce their teachers, teachers

To denounce each other. Badger, confuse, demoralize,
Browbeat, terrorize—stay icy calm yourself,
Increase your power.

When I saw such things
In our small county seat, and pictured them
In counties to left and right, above and below,
I was ready to believe no man could escape
Such a net. They made the meshes daily smaller.

The Learner

A teacher returned to Changchow after three months' brainwashing.
"I learned something in Foochow," he said. "I learned
How to express myself. It's not so much
What your opinion is nowadays. People have
All sorts of opinions, and no one knows more than another
If yours is the right one or not. It's how you express it.
Assume the right air, use the right jargon, clothe
Yourself in irreproachable motives, and no one
Will attempt to oppose you. Guidance from the top
Doesn't cover much territory. I go ahead
With what I think is right, but I take a leaf
Out of their book and find first an acceptable reason.

"The other day some students came to me
With a patriotic proposal. In two of the classrooms
We have desks and seats imported from the United States,
The best desks and seats we have. They proposed to destroy them,
Burn the wood, smash the cast-iron frames,
And thereby demonstrate contempt for America.

"Well, I'm acting dean now. I knew there was no one
Of those above me who wanted those desks destroyed.
Who would replace them? But how could I dissuade

Those boys without drawing their attention to me?
I said, 'It's true those desks come from the rotten Americans
And it would be a pleasure to destroy them.
But think! Our army uses American trucks,
American arms, American clothes—the spoils of war.
They laugh at Americans, they say, "Thank you, silly fools,
We'll use your own weapons to humble you." Look here!
Not only these measly benches, these buildings, this lab equipment
Are gifts from Americans, part of their two-faced policy,
Their cultural invasion, their slick imperialism.
Shall we burn the buildings, smash the equipment? How stupid!
We'd be more stupid than they were when they thought
They could bribe us with gifts and exploit us. Let's be clever,
Use these gifts, these imperialistic attempts
At bribery; but, like the army, use them
For our own purposes, for our own People's Democracy.' "

"Don't make a slip," said Hank.

"Don't worry," he said,
"After three months in Foochow I can reel this stuff off in my sleep."

The Prospect

Sim's son had been head of his class at school,
But he kept running a fever, and the doctor
Told Sim to keep him at home and make him rest.
So the boy missed the last few months and didn't graduate.
He could have been valedictorian.

"How he reads!"
Said Sim. "He always reads books; he never grows tired.
He lies in bed upstairs and reads all day,
Big books, not children's books. He knows more characters

Than most of the teachers."

"Too bad he had to drop out,"
I said. "Do you think he will enter middle school
This fall?"

"I doubt it," said Sim, "but, after all,
What if he doesn't? What will middle school give him?
Propaganda—anti-religious, anti-Christian.
What can he look forward to? The smarter he is,
The more we can be sure the State will grab him,
Take special pains to indoctrinate him, instill
Aversion for and suspicion of his family,
Isolate him from friends, from all local influences,
And make of him a dehumanized tool or weapon.
I'd just as soon have him stay in bed and read books."

Hush!

The preacher never talked politics in his sermons.
It wasn't that he ignored the Communists
Nor had no opinion about their regime, nor even
Because he was afraid of them (he was afraid);
But because he was so intent on preaching the Bible.
He never varied: Bible story—explanation.
His religious and moral applications of the stories
Were timeless, had no topical references, advocated
Conduct and principles which the most depraved
Approve in theory, complaining only that good people
Don't practice what they preach.

Out of the pulpit,
He was startlingly outspoken about the Reds,
And his wife used to worry. At our house one day

He was telling us some thing about the school cadre.
"What liars those fellows are," he said, "what liars!
They lie to teachers, to students, to everyone! It's a policy.
They lie all the time."

"Not so loud, not so loud!" said his wife.
She was afraid to let him out of her sight.

They were shooting people two or three times a week then;
Some executions were public and some secret.
One day he and I had to go to the bank together,
And on the way we saw the death sentences posted
With **X** in vermilion ink at the top of each placard
To show that the person or persons listed had been
Condemned to death. He went over and read them all.
"Here's a high school teacher," he said, "and here's another.
Here's the chairman of the board of such-and-such school."
He picked out all the educated people
And turned away with a sigh. We went to the bank.

Reassurance

Our house-woman was a Christian. "Last night," she said,
"My sister-in-law and her little boy were in town
And were passing the church when the boy gave a cry of fear.
My sister-in-law looked up. At the gate of the church,
Majestic, tall, taller than the gateway itself,
She saw a spirit standing. And she herself was afraid,
Too afraid to speak. They crept by and came up here.

"Now, she's not a Christian. She doesn't know about angels;
She couldn't connect an angel with the church.
But when I heard her, I knew what it was. In these days,
God has set His angel here to protect His own."

A Conservative

Lian had been principal of the Mission primary school
For twenty-two or twenty-three years. He retired
And went into business. He did very well in business,
Loaned money at interest, and bought some fields.
He was a good man, an elder in the church,
But stern and set in his ways. He was on the board
Of the primary school, and often in board meetings
Would recall for the principal's benefit the wonderful days
When the Mission had sole control and he had been principal.
No government registration then, no school board,
Just missionary and principal doing the best job possible:
Equipment complete, building always in good repair,
A dedicated faculty, and a docile student body.

Lian didn't think much of the Nationalists. But when they left
And the Communists were coming, he assembled his family
And said, "Prepare your hearts for dark days to come.
I'm putting my affairs in the best shape possible.
I expect trouble, and I want us all to be ready."
Then he read the Bible and prayed with them.
One of his tenants brought accusations against him
As an unjust landlord. His fields were confiscated
And he was arrested and sentenced to hard labor.
He worked on the road they were building outside the city.
Members of the family would go out and stand
By the side of the road as he was marched out or in,
Not all of them on the same day, two or three at a time,
And they would exchange a glance with him.

                    One day they saw
A notice accusing him of the usual crimes
And giving his sentence, death. When the day came
For him and his group, the whole family lined the road

And, as he passed, they thought he fixed his gaze
On each of them with more than the usual meaning.
They wondered if he knew what was going to happen.

One of his nieces, a nurse, went out to the field
After the execution and found his body;
It had been cut almost in two by machine-gun bullets.
She said he had had a good meal. She saw the rice.

Tribute to the Sims

"She brings you through the doorway, and he feeds you,"
Said a girl who had been converted by the Sims.

They could have gone to Taiwan or to Burma
And taken charge of an established school, but they felt
That God had called them to Leng-na, this up-country town,
To begin work among girls, the first Church middle school
In our district.

The preacher, who had come to Leng-na with them
And who taught math in the school, was appalled by the girls
At first and called them wild horses and wild geese,
Noisy, rough, with none of the city graces.
They were almost all non-Christians, some of them
Facing difficult problems in their families.
"But one thing about these girls," said Sim, "they know
How to work. They've worked from childhood, carried water
And other burdens, cleaned the house, helped in the fields.
They expect to work, and we give them work to do here
Around the school, and standards of work, and we tell them
That work is good, and relate it to service for God."

Everyone in the school became conscious of God.
With the Sims He was always present, always consulted,

And He became real to others, became the Helper
In daily life and daily cares—and the cares
That oppressed the girls weren't always such simple ones.
But they were all brought out and laid before God with prayer.
Past sins, present failures and perplexities
Were burdens cast upon God, a daily faring forth
At the side of God, and a joy in His unfailing
Companionship and help.

In their household,
It was almost impossible to doubt God, to reject
His love revealed in Christ. Could they doubt the Sims?
Their day's routine gleamed with the love of Christ.

They heard people say they couldn't understand
What the minister preached on Sunday, they had no grounding,
So they started a Saving Grace Committee, designed
To make the Gospel simple, spell it out,
Make way in people's hearts for thoughtful hearing
Of Sunday worship. Past ten weeks of this,
The preacher took them over and prepared them
For church membership. For the first time there was
A steady stream of new members into the church.

Came the comrades, Sim was a marked man. Anyone
Who knew his record would know that the Reds wouldn't like him.
He was too smart and too honest. At university,
Though he was at the head of his class, his diploma
Was held up because he refused military training
And declared pacifism to be the Christian position.
On Kulangsu during the war, the Japanese
Tolerated his scruples, made him superintendent
Of schools, and let him tell the truth as he saw it
So long as he did his job of education.

A colleague, one with similar experience,
Wrote him, "This job, under our present rulers,
Is ten times harder than under the Japanese."

From the first the Reds had their eyes on our girls' middle school
And would try Sim out this way and that way. He was correct
In his answers, trying to follow regulations,
But they knew he had no sympathy with them,
And was trying his best to keep them out of the school.

Sim used to study all the documents promulgated
By Peking and Foochow. If the Reds interfered
In the school or requested him or the school to do something
Beyond the letter of their authority, Sim
Refused, and cited their rules to them, line upon line.
In chapel talks and in Sunday morning sermons
He stressed probity and honor, and his stories
And parables brought out many a smile. Said a friend,
"Tan has no trouble, he preaches the pure Bible story,
But the words Sim uses have bones in them, and he's done for."
The last talk I heard Sim give, he said, "Gold is gold.
Pile dung on top and claim it's all dung, but the gold
Is still gold."

The Reds went after the students,
Urging them to accuse Sim or his wife or some teachers,
But the students wouldn't budge. The Reds approached the teachers.
The teachers were solid. Well, perhaps a trifle shaky,
But none would accuse Sim of anything.

Then a request
Came from Foochow for each private school to send
One of its teaching staff there for three months' training.
We sent a woman, a Christian, a sweet girl, but—
She was vulnerable. She had a relative

Who had been a member of the Provincial Council
Under the Nationalists. He had made his peace
With the Communists and was at large, but still,
Anytime they wanted to, they could clap him in jail.

When she returned home she became their spy in the school.
She had to make daily reports of all activities
And of the school situation. Sim knew about this
And was careful. But the object of the Reds
Was to put him in a situation where *any*
Choice he made was a bad one for him. The girl
Proposed that they organize in school a committee
To support an activity of the government
Which Sim thought was pernicious. "Yet," he said,
"She takes a patriotic stand in proposing it,
And I, if I refuse, am unpatriotic.
But, if I accede, I feel I am doing wrong."

While they bored this way from within, a man from Amoy
Was made principal of the government middle school,
A man whom Sim had discharged as incompetent
In Amoy twelve years before. This man hated Sim
And made it his main objective to bring Sim down.
He was in Leng-na for a year. When the Party moved
Against Sim, he had been transferred to Tingchow,
But gladly returned to make his accusations.

Thirteen years before, in Amoy, Sim had edited
An alumni paper. One issue of it contained
An article by someone else denouncing
Communism. The accusations were based on this.
The man who unearthed this material was Sim's enemy.
They were ready. A joint meeting of the teachers'
And the students' organizations was called, and Sim
Was attacked as unpatriotic. His students were urged

To accuse him. They were silent. Other students
Rose up and attacked him vehemently. *Our* students wept.
Then two of them rose and spoke in defense of Sim
As truly patriotic, better than his accusers.
They were shouted down, and our group broke into sobs,
But they were steadfast.

The girl who had spied on Sim
Was not made to accuse him. She gave information.
Other teachers from other schools rose up now
To accuse Sim of various things—lack of patriotism,
Collaboration with Japan, friendship with Americans,
Making students afraid by retailing to them
The propaganda heard on the Voice of America broadcasts.
This went on for two days.

Sim was sick at heart.
The charge that he was unpatriotic hurt the most.
"I love my country," he said, "I want her true welfare."
He decided it was best for the school for him
To resign, go away. We tried, the board tried, to dissuade him,
But he was convinced that he must, that otherwise
The Reds would attack the board, the school, through him.
If he got out, the school might have a chance.
We hadn't the slightest hope of improvement
If he got out; the object of the Communists
Was to get him out so they could take over the school.
But the board accepted Sim's resignation, and he
Applied for a pass to return with his family to Kulangsu.

There was a lull of about a week, and then
One night we went down the hill for a special meeting
At which Sim was supposed to speak. As we neared the church,
We heard moaning sounds, moaning and terrible wailing,
From one of the Sunday-school rooms. "What on earth is that?"

Joyce asked. The preacher's wife said, "Sim is gone,
And some students are praying to God for his safe return."
"But what has happened to Sim?" A deacon said,
"Two soldiers came to his house this afternoon
And asked him to come with them to the station house
To pick up his travel pass. He went with them
But he hasn't come back. No one knows where he is."
As others came to the church, there was a hubbub.
Then men who'd been sent out came back with word
Sim was in the local jail.

                    A man in the cell
With Sim was released a few days later. He said
That Sim was reading and writing all the time.
The Reds were asking him for his written opinion
Of certain books. They had also asked him to write
His autobiography. Everything he wrote
Was returned to him time after time for revision. We knew then
They were trying to brainwash him.

                    A few weeks later
His wife was aroused by police at eleven p.m.
She was told, "You are being accused by other teachers.
You must come and defend yourself." The preacher's wife
In the other half of the house came over to help her,
And advised her to make her defense. She helped her dress,
And Mrs. Sim disappeared also. Again it was
A cellmate who brought us news. Mrs. Sim, she said,
Was preaching to the women in her cell.

A new principal was appointed by the government,
And the school board, for the second time, was reorganized,
"To eliminate reactionary elements
And to incorporate progressive elements."
Nothing drastic was done. The new principal

Was a good man, his wife was a Christian; the new board members
Were good men, too. The point was, the Reds had control.
That was enough for the moment. The rest could wait.

Public executions took place twice a week,
Fifteen or twenty were shot each time. We could see them
Led past the church and out of the North Gate
To the execution grounds. People would pass
Our house and run to the point of our ridge to look down
On the spectacle from a safe distance. The secret shootings
Took place somewhere outside the East Gate.

One day
The rumor went around that Sim had been executed;
Someone said he had seen Sim led past the church.
One of the members said, "I was so upset,
I went out and looked at every corpse. Thank the Lord!
Mr. Sim wasn't there."

When we left China at Easter,
Sim and his wife were still in the local jail.

A Note on Prayer

Said the preacher, "What do you do with a man who has lungs
And doesn't breathe? You carry him out and bury him."

Somebody Else, Not Me

Our relations with the police were friendly. Wally
Had gone ahead of us and the procedure
Had been established. Although they were alert
To every word we spoke to them, in general,
They trusted us. After we had received a letter

Telling us our exit permits were granted,
We wanted to see the police to make arrangements
For our departure. We looked around for someone
To act as interpreter. No one wanted to go.

Some of the men had been to the station with us
On other occasions, but now, several times a week
The Reds were shooting people, and these same police
Were the ones who had to get ready the paraphernalia
And carry out the sentences. "Just go on down,"
They said to us, "those men understand some Amoy.
You'll get along all right."

So we went. One policeman
Kept talking along in Mandarin, I nodding my head.
"Do you understand me, pastor?" he asked. He smiled.
"I'm afraid you don't."

He spoke slowly then, and together
We worked out the arrangements for our exit.

GLOSSARY

Change

Good News

For a Biblical analog to the prisoner's story, see Acts 16:23-40. The blessings in Isaiah 61:1 and Luke 4:18-19 are also relevant.

preacher

A non-ordained native evangelist.

round, round, round

This style of repetition is typical of southern Chinese narrative; each successive iteration receives less vocal emphasis. Rhetorically, it denotes a weariness of the topic in the storyteller—this is the "same old story," told once more to disbelievers.

the Manchu dynasty

Or the Chi'ng (Qing) dynasty. This series of emperors of Mongol origin superseded the Ming dynasty, ruling from 1644 through 1912. The years to 1799 are regarded as a golden age in imperial administration.

his great chair which requires eight bearers

A ceremonial sedan chair or palanquin, carried through the streets by a team of servants.

Luck

Soa^n-sia^n

Present-day Shenchangzhen.

bandits

Countryside bandits flourished in South Fukien through World War II by taxing villagers, robbing highway-traveling merchants, kidnapping for ransom, and extortion by direct threat or through a note of demand. Like Western organized crime figures, some took tribute in exchange for ridding a region of its lesser criminals. To ward off any alerting of government soldiers, some trumpeted their family connections to church members, and appeased missionaries by giving in to demands for better treatment of the people. The three main bandit groups in the Mission territory were headquartered outside Changchow (Zhangzhou), at An-khoe (Anqi), and in the West River country north of Sio-khe (Shange).

a two-dime piece

Worth two-tenths of the value of the period Chinese dollar.

He Taketh the Wise

I Corinthians 3:19—"For the wisdom of this world is foolishness with God. For it is written, He taketh the wise in their own craftiness." See also Job 5:13.

cash by cash

A *cash* is a thin brass coin, slightly over an inch in diameter, with a square center hole allowing it to be threaded on a string for banking.

Cheaper

pastor

An ordained native minister placed in charge of a church and native congregation.

Behold My Lord

Uncle John

Not Angus's uncle, but his missionary predecessor, an "Old China Hand" to relative newcomers. Western names in the edition belong to missionary characters.

our grand old man

An elder Chinese pastor.

To serve his Master and to bring His kingdom here

As John the Baptist served the Savior: "This is [he], of whom it is written, Behold, I send my messenger before thy face, which shall prepare thy way before thee." (Luke 7:27; see also Matthew 11:10.)

Synod

A regional assembly and church judicial body consisting of native pastors and missionaries delegated by the district Classes (q.v. *classis*). The Synod of South Fukien was created in 1894 by the Reformed and English Presbyterian missionaries; the London Missionary Society joined in 1920.

Holdout

chapel

As opposed to a church, a chapel was a worship building whose attendees were too few to support it financially. It was maintained by Mission funds, and supervised by a preacher or an itinerant missionary moderator (q.v.) rather than a resident pastor.

A Grandfather

the girls' middle school

A "middle school" taught secondary education.

consistory

The governing body of a local church, composed of its pastor and installed elders.

the Little Flock

A movement of holier-than-thou fundamentalists whose members proselytized aggressively among Amoy Mission converts, causing division and annoying the poet.

Girls

and when she can, / She'll take a girl into the house for him

Chinese families frequently exchanged girl babies, on the assumption that an arranged marriage is better than other choices, as the parents have control over whom their sons marry, and in the long run can "train" a daughter- in-law to serve them when they are old and dependent. The custom also assumes that sons will be more loyal to the family, as breadwinners and as inheritors of the family name and traditions. Thus, sons are assets, and girls are liabilities. Chinese parents worked very hard at establishing and maintaining these ties. Infanticide is a practical strategy in families that are wretchedly poor, a practicing of euthanasia, especially when there is "no food."

Safe

They're going to give them away

To the horror of Westerners, Chinese peasant culture—oppressed by poverty and shaped by folk renderings of Confucian and Buddhist teachings—allowed the infanticide of female children or their later sale as bondservants or child fiancées.

Big Sister

Classis

A district assembly and judicial body consisting of native pastors, church elders, and missionaries. Equivalent to a Presbyterian Church *presbytery.* In Mandarin, *tai-hoey,* "great assembly."

An Illustration

Late March: West River Road

a haze / Of early mist

The road would have led to or followed the West River (Xi Qi), to the northeast of Sio-khe.

kwa

Possibly *Rhus chinensis,* Chinese gall or sumac. The "ruddy" new leaves are a political allusion.

The bamboos are like pale and stooped old men

A common Chinese rhetorical trope was the advice that individual survival through changing times depends on bending and not breaking, like the bamboo.

Cherokees

Rosa laevigata, or Cherokee rose, a climbing rose with a fragrant white blossom.

opium

In the warlord era a punitive tax on crop fields made the growing of opium almost mandatory for the survival of farmers' families; Angus passed dozens of opium fields in the countryside around Sio-khe, c. 1926. With the coming to power of the Nationalists the growing was officially outlawed, though Angus knew of one corrupt general who, through Chiang Kai-shek's (Jiang Jieshi's) politic tolerance, had it continued in South Fukien for his own profit. Other accounts have Chiang's government actively supporting the opium trade, which would have subsidized Nationalist forces as readily as bandit armies.

Unrest

Not Ashamed

When the Nationalists came through in '26

As the introduction details, an allied force of Nationalist and Communist armies under the Kuomintang (Guomindang) party, or KMT, occupied Fukien on its Northern Expedition route toward the capture of Nanking (Nanjing). The anti-Western events described in the poem were instigated by the Communists, but were tolerated, or even better regarded, by many among the Nationalist faction.

The people were given Sun Yat-sen for their saint

Almost literally; in 1927 the KMT government, in part to appease the then allied Communists, importuned the Synod of South Fukien to instate at the Mission schools weekly memorial ceremonies for Sun, which would include bows made to his portrait. The request was denied, its spirit seeming too akin to worship.

running dogs

A slur denoting subservience used by both Nationalists and the Chinese Communist Party (CCP) to condemn foreign-accommodating Chinese, seen as lackeys to imperialism. After Mao Tse-tung's (Mao Zedong's) Cultural Revolution began in 1966, the phrase entered American political discourse through the slogans of the leftist element on college campuses.

"Let him speak!" yelled the crowd, delighted

For many among the public at this date, if not for the organizers and their victim, such a political event was an entertainment—a kind of imposed street theater irrelevant under transient authority. Still, having CCP-affiliated troops militant in Fukien produced loose cadres of *thaw-kiong*, or civilian communists, outspoken against foreign organizations in China.

a revolutionist

In context of the times, a proponent of republican nationalism, and thus ostensibly a former supporter of Sun.

Toast Refused

Occupied Chapel

you could take it up in Changchow / Or with your consul

The chapel at Lam-khi^{n} (modern name uncertain) was an outstation of the church at Changchow; as the chapel's moderator, Reverend Angus could appeal the matter to the Changchow Classis. The regional American consular office was located in the international settlement on Kulangsu (q.v.) The *consul* would be the U.S. diplomatic representative, protector of American trade and political interests, and of the rights of U.S. citizens.

Able to Give

The title phrase occurs in Scripture to denote that sacrifice must be apportioned according to the resources of the sacrificer; see Deuteronomy 16:17, Ezekiel 46:5. An analog to the action of the congregation in the poem occurs in II Chronicles 25:1-9. Amiziah, ruler of the tribes of Israel, questions how he will regain the hundred talents spent to purchase an army God has directed him not to use. He disregards the expense when a prophet assures him that "The Lord is able to give thee much more than this."

an ancestral hall

Worship building devoted to veneration of ancestral shrines, and thus unseemly to use for Christian worship—though Reformed Church missionaries did not discourage converts from ordinary family memorials. And, as "Bible Woman's Report" shows, of necessity outstation worship buildings sometimes did double duty.

The Tiger's Things

the brief southeast revolt

In November 1933 a coalition of military commanders of Kwangsi (Guangxi) and Kwangtung (Guangdong) provinces, based in Canton (Guangzhou), organized a rebellion against the Nanking government and set up an alternate People's Government in Fukien. The rebels called for Chiang Kai-shek's overthrow, and for a united front of KMT and CCP forces to press war upon Japan. The insurrection was quashed in January 1934. The revolt and its instigators, the "Cantonese," are referred to in several poems of Angus's *Unrest* section.

Moderator

Outstation chapels and churches without a native preacher or pastor were monitored by a missionary moderator, who visited to give the sacraments and lend administrative aid.

he sent some . . . things

Presumably munitions.

The Tiger, The Bull, and The Fox

the London Mission part

The area of the Changchow Classis purview ministered to by members of the London [England] Missionary Society, a predominantly Congregationalist organization operating in South Fukien since 1844.

kidnapped by actors

In childhood the Fox was kidnapped by a troupe of traveling actors, presumably to supply them with a servant or a boy player.

Black Bills

black bills

Extortion notes delivered by a bandit gang, or "Blacks."

A Favor

Foochow (Fuzhou)

The provincial capital of Fukien.

I cut the caper

Anglo-American phrase for "making mischief," in print as early as *Twelfth Night*, and here a believable between-the-wars slang rendering of "*I* make the moves here."

After the Looting

Communist forces briefly occupying Changchow in 1932 took the missionary compound for their headquarters. The Anguses' possessions were looted as imperialist booty and "redistributed" to the people in a public park.

But I shall do again / What I repent now

Amid a lament echoing the Psalms, a nod to St. Paul in Romans 7:15-19.

where the treasure is

Matthew 6:21; Luke 12:34. See also Matthew 12:35.

Must we eat wind again?

A native plaint heard in the event of crop failure or financial loss.

The Arm

The 19th Route Army revolted in '33

The Nineteenth Route Army of the KMT defended Shanghai against Japanese attack from January through May 1932. After a truce was made, Chiang Kai-shek—who distrusted the army's commander—sent these troops to Fukien to drive out insurgent communist forces. Once in command in the south, the Nineteenth Route Army's leaders allied with the southern rebel commanders who created the People's Government at Fukien. When the revolt was overcome the army was returned to KMT control and renamed. Once its revolutionary presence was gone, some Fukienese expressed a preference for the Nineteenth Route Army's behavior over that of the "loyal" Nationalist troops that replaced it.

Nationalist planes flew down and bombed Changchow

At this time an urban center of insurrection in Fukien. Changchow's Mission, civic, and civilian property would again suffer bombing by the Japanese, as well as occupation damage.

I chased them into the street

Compare with Jesus' injunction in Matthew 18:5-6.

Communists

There's Thah-tham . . . / . . . Toa-khe on our side

The villages named first in these lines were Reformed Church outstations on the western side of the range of hills used as a hide-out by the uncertain "communists" of the poem.

Changpu and Un-sio

Zhangbu and Yunxiao, on the eastern side of the hills, were outstations of the English Presbyterian mission.

Mandarin

The standard language of China, as opposed to regional dialects, of which Fukien alone was once thought to have over one hundred..

the salt gabelle

A central government system which licensed individuals to collect the salt tax. The revenues were applied to the China's detested debts to foreign corporations.

The Cantonese we have now are pretty clever

"White" troops commanded by Cantonese loyal to the Nanking government.

I don't think this crowd are real Reds at all

If the kidnappers discussed by the characters in the poem were Communists, they would be unregimented guerrillas or renegades whose politics were uncertain. The arrival of the pre-revolt Nineteenth Route Army in 1933, and Chiang's subsequent "Bandit Suppression Campaigns," forced CCP armies to retire to the Kiangsi (Jiangxi) Soviet, a mountain stronghold overlapping the provincial border of Kiangsi and Fukien. The armies' 1934 "Long March" to shelter in the far northwest left behind only reserve bands ordered to maintain some encampments in the Chiang-beseiged Soviet, which was far from the Mission territory.

the Reds up north have shown the way

Presumably those holdouts of the Kiangsi Soviet compelled to surrender by 1936, the "present" of the poem. Angus was aware that the Reds that held the city of Leng-na (Longyan) and the surrounding countryside to the nearer north from 1928 to 1932 had been forced to retreat to Kiangsi. But the actions of every Red band cannot be accounted for.

when the Communists took power / They executed Pastor Tiu^{n}

He had been an informant to the Nationalists in earlier years.

Christmas Story

Chiu Hok-tek

A mythical character of antiquity. A politicized hagiography would likewise accompany the rise to power of Mao Tse-tung.

War

Ground All Cleared

A Call on the Fox

Why We Forgot

Chungking means Chiang Kai-shek

Prior to the Japanese capture of Nanking in December 1937, Chiang's national government retired to Chungking (Chongqing) in the province of Szechwan (Sichuan), far from the fighting front.

Wang Ching-wei

In March 1940 the Japanese made the disaffected vice-president of the KMT head of a puppet government in occupied Nanking. An early revolutionist, once an ally of Sun Yat-sen and, less certainly, of Chang Kai-shek, Wang held unlikely hopes of prevailing in authority once the Japanese presence receded from northern China.

Kulangsu (Gulangyu)

Or "the Drum-wave Island," located near the mainland, a half-mile southwest of Amoy Island. It had been a Mission site since 1842, eventually incorporating successful schools and hospitals.

the International Settlement

One of many territorial concessions made to Westerners by treaty, removed from Chinese jurisdiction and reserved for foreign commercial, residential, and diplomatic use.

The Japanese stopped all the launches

In the fall of 1941, in retribution for the assassination of an official on the island.

the Japanese bombed Talmage College again

Named for forty-year missionary John Van Nest Talmage, this institution combined "middle" and post-secondary education in a union effort of the Reformed and Presbyterian missions. Its post-secondary program was soon dropped due to success in placing middle school graduates at Fukien's other Christian colleges and theological seminary. The college was relocated from Kulangsu to Changchow in 1925. From 1938 through the war years it was removed to the up-country village of Hoa-an (Huaan), but there did not escape Japanese bombing runs as hoped. Sited on a hill as it was, the effect of the Japanese attack on an American institution was a lesson to Changchow.

Big Rapids

On the North River (Jiulong Jiang) in Fukien Province.

Don Bell

American radio news correspondent of the period, heard in U.S.-friendly cities throughout the Pacific.

the Prince of Wales and the Repulse

British battleship and battle cruiser, respectively. News of their sinking off Malaya by Japanese planes reached the Chinese mainland by December 10, 1941 (east China time).

Like Water

the Romanized

A printed phonetic rendering in the Latin alphabet of words as spoken in the Amoy dialect, used to teach the Scriptures and communicate news to the many Mission-territory Chinese who could not read Chinese characters.

the government wants to arrest them

A common sight in towns during the war years was marching troops leading to the front files of conscripts tied together to keep them from escaping. Many died on these forced journeys.

Death of the Fox

silver

One of the favorite currencies of the Chinese, it was frequently hoarded and buried. The circumstances of the Bull's calling in the people's silver ahead of the government's wartime demands suggest the parable of the unprofitable servant, punished for burying the talents his master gave him instead of letting them circulate and increase. (Matthew 25:14-30).

Death of the Tiger

the Chekiang front

In mid-1942 Japan advanced its occupation line from the northern China territory seized in 1937–1938 to central Chekiang (Zhejiang), the province on Fukien's northeastern border.

the English Presbyterians

Evangelical and organizational co-operants with the Reformed Church in South Fukien since 1850.

Lotus

Bible woman

A woman preacher, educated in Mission schools, who evangelized among single ladies.

The Japanese took Singapore

Allied forces there surrendered on February 15, 1942.

Thunderstruck

Anatomy Lesson

the days of Tiu^{n} Ge

As a lesser bandit commander under the warlord of Shanghai, Tiu^{n} Ge controlled a region that encompassed the cities of Sio-khe (near present-day Pinghe), Changchow, and Tong-an (Tongan), until driven out by Nationalist troops in 1926.

Good Friday

The couplets recall those of "The Lie," by Donne's contemporary, Walter Raleigh, and the tenor of Angus's poem bears comparison.

The Shooting

After He had Sung a Hymn

Cf. Matthew 26:30, the progress to the Mount of Olives after the Last Supper.

Then I made my bed on some boards laid across two benches

Angus's hosts were often amused to find him too tall for Chinese beds. The boards provided him harbored bedbugs nonetheless.

Inflation

Prodigal

the younger son

The parable of the prodigal son resonates deeply in a land where fidelity to the family is highly esteemed. As the Angus poems show, many families had a relative who proved headstrong or a wastrel, and later found redemption, or did not. (Some of these "bad sons" became bandits, or took pay to spot victims for them.) The contrasting example of Joseph illustrates the Chinese ideal of husbandry.

Distance

Measure for Measure

Compare Jesus' lesson in Luke 6:37-38.

two catties on every measure

The *catty,* as a measure of rice, varies depending on the county or locale where used. The standard mainland catty is generally equal to about 1.33 pounds or

0.59 kilograms. Pastors' salaries were often paid in rice, more stable in value than paper money—so a short measure made quite a difference.

Profit for God

Like the apostle

Paul, in Philippians 4:12.

down from Hopeh

Hebei, the northeastern province dominated by Peking (Beijing), the imperial capital and later that of the PRC as well. Alternately transliterated on pre-Pinyin maps as *Hopei.*

I joined Feng Yu-hsiang's army

A northern warlord since 1914, Feng became a power broker in the long struggle toward nationalism by virtue of his alliances with, and disaffection for, various rising and falling military leaders and political movements. The sincerity of his faith, in practice, is variously reported. Feng closed his career by electing absorption into the People's Republic of China's military ranks, and was lost in a shipwreck while on a mission to the Soviet Union.

I was baptized along with a lot of others

In his heyday, Feng, the "Christian general," was known for baptizing his troops *en masse*—using fire hoses.

a hundred coppers

A "copper" is a coin made mostly of that metal, about 1.25 inches in diameter, with a fluctuating value.

Rescue

The An-hai launch

A small steamboat carrying passengers to and from the town of An-hai (Anhai), on a coastal inlet northeast of Amoy Island.

The Three Trees

The title suggests the three crosses on Golgotha. The poem's brigands have not profited from the example of the good thief (Luke 23:40-43).

All Smoothed Over

Incident on the Road

Advance Rumors

beef is cheaper

The people commonly ate pork and chicken. Beef was from dray animals—water buffalo, oxen, or red bullocks—slaughtered only when unfit for further labor.

A Warning

In the days of Sung

The Sung (Song) dynasty ruled from 960 through 1126. It reunited China under a central government after earlier divisions, but was overrun in the north, surviving as the Southern Sung (Song) dynasty, 1127–1279.

as we worshipped idols our bodies got smaller

Household idols were commonly less than three feet tall. *Cf.*, however, the view on political iconography in "Not Ashamed," in the time that monumentalist portraiture was on the rise: "When the Nationalists came through in '26, / The people were given Sun Yat-sen for their saint, / And his picture was in every public building."

A Caution

Bible Woman's Report

Her story is perhaps an analog of the missionary experience in China.

bracken stored for fuel

A large, hardy fern that, once cut and dried, burns with a thick, acrid, eye-stinging smoke.

Communists

Valley Landscape, Sin-kio

Sin-kio (Xinkou) was near the northern boundary of the Mission territory, far from Leng-na, the district center.

the burned-over hillside

Yearly, farmers burned the dry cover from the hills, partly to reduce the rodent population.

pride-of-India

Probably the Chinaberry, *Melia azedarach*, genus *Meliaceae*, which produces clusters of red berries.

oil-plant

Probably rapeseed *(Brassica napus).*

balks

Unplowed strips of earth left as boundaries in farmers' fields.

a trembling flood of color

I.e., red. Duckweed: *lemnaceae.*

ENTHUSIAST

fired by Sung's preaching

Dr. John Sung, a dramatic revival leader educated in America, was active in his native Fukien in the mid-1930s. His preaching invoked nationalist ideals, and frequently anti-Western sentiments.

Seminary

The South Fukien Theological Seminary, like Talmage College a mission union institution. The seminary also relocated from Kulangsu to Changchow, but in the prewar years instead retreated to another North River district village, Eng-hok (Yongfu).

THE STUDENT MIND

Chinese students would be accustomed to rote learning *en groupe,* with punishment for varying from the text. The poem, however, may present an allegory of incoming learning styles.

AN EXCEEDING WEIGHT OF GLORY

II Corinthians 4:17, "For our light affliction, which is but for a moment, worketh for us a far more exceeding [and] eternal weight of glory."

THE LEARNER

I learned something in Foochow

By 1950 the site of an indoctrination center for Fukienese regarded as not wholeheartedly embracing communism.

THE PROSPECT

he knows more characters / Than most of the teachers

Only China's most accomplished scholars knew all of the written language's ideograms. Ordinary literates got by using only a few hundred characters.

Hush!

Reassurance

A Conservative

Tribute to the Sims

The name *Sim* translates as "heart" or "spirit." The William R. Angus, Jr. Collection at the Joint Archives of Holland contains photographs of the Sim family and an Angus interview transcript featuring comments on their bravery.

university

The interdenominational Fukien Christian University, at Foochow.

Voice of America broadcasts

American radio programs extolling democratic ideals, beamed to Asian countries, Eastern Europe, and like "trouble spots" to discourage adherence to communism.

A Note on Prayer

In his post-China years Angus added to the finalized arrangement ofhis complete China poems several two-line verses inspired by anecdotes remembered. One humorous example was titled "Ideographic": "Said Clarence, 'Did you scratch up my piano like that?' / Said the moving-man, 'I don't know how to write!' "

Somebody Else, Not Me

The apostle Peter betrayed Christ in words similar to the title phrase. (Matthew 26:69-75; Mark 14:66-72; John 18:15-27; Luke 22:54-62.)

talking along in Mandarin

The imperial administrative language was retained as such in the People's Republic of China, a utilitarian decision that enhanced the air of historical appropriateness assumed by the new Peking-based government.

BIBLIOGRAPHY

Books

Borg, Dorothy. *American Policy and the Chinese Revolution, 1925–1928.* New York: American Institute of Pacific Relations and the Macmillan Company, 1947.

Buruma, Ian. *Bad Elements: Chinese Rebels from Los Angeles to Beijing.* New York: Random House, 2001.

Ching, Julia. *Probing China's Soul: Religion, Politics and Protest in the People's Republic.* San Francisco: Harper & Row, 1990.

Clubb, O. Edmund. *Twentieth Century China.* New York and London: Columbia University Press, 1964.

De Jong, Gerald F. *The Reformed Church in China 1842-1951,* The Historical Series of the Reformed Church in America, No. 22. Grand Rapids, MI: The Wm. B. Eerdmans Publishing Company, 1992.

Fairbank, John King. *Trade and Diplomacy on the China Coast: The Opening of the Treaty Ports 1842–1854,* 2 vols. Cambridge, MA: Harvard University Press, 1953.

—, ed. *The Missionary Experience in China and America,* Harvard Studies in American-East Asian Relations. Cambridge, MA: Harvard University Press, 1974.

Hsü, Immanuel C. Y. *The Rise of Modern China.* New York: Oxford University Press, 1970.

Johnson, Paul. *Modern Times: The World from the Twenties to the Eighties.* New York: Harper Collins, 1983.

Latourette, Kenneth S. *A History of Christian Missions in China.* New Haven: Yale University Press, 1929; reprint, New York: Russell & Russell, 1967.

Lutz, Jessie G., ed. *Christian Missions in China: Evangelists of What?* Problems in Asian Civilizations Series. Boston: D. C. Heath & Company, 1965.

Spence, Jonathan D. *The Search for Modern China.* New York and London: W. W. Norton & Company, 1990.

Terrill, Ross. *China in Our Time.* New York: Simon & Schuster, 1992.

Tuchman, Barbara. *Stillwell and the American Experience in China, 1911-45.* New York: The Macmillan Company, 1971.

Twitchett, Denis, and John King Fairbank, gen. eds. *The Cambridge History of China,* vols. 12-15. Cambridge: Cambridge University Press, 1983-1991

Varg, Paul A. *Missionaries, Chinese and Diplomats: The American Protestant Missionary Movement in China, 1890-1952*. Princeton: Princeton University Press, 1958.

Articles

Angus, William R., Jr. "Country Pastors in China." *Intelligencer-Leader,* 1 April 1938.

—. "The Tiger, The Bull, and The Fox." *Intelligencer-Leader,* 28 January 1938.

—. "Two Friends of Evangelism." *Intelligencer-Leader,* 10 June 1938.

Van Wyk, Gordon J. "Missions and Nationalism." *Western Seminary Bulletin* 5:4 (March 1952).

Lectures

Angus, William R., Jr. "Talks on Religious Poetry." Delivered at Baguio, Philippines, 1961 and 1965. Typescript, Angus Family collection.

Interviews

Angus, William R., Jr. Interviews by David M. Vander Haar, tape recordings and transcripts, 16-17 September 1976. The Old China Hands Oral History Project, Joint Archives of Holland, Holland, MI.

About the Editors

David Angus is the son of missionary poet William Angus. He is a retired educator and the author of "The Many Roles of Harry Lewis: A Study of Motive and Method in Creative Technique," a dissertation that addresses the influence of a lifelong identity crisis on Sinclair Lewis's early career as a novelist.

David Andrews is an independent scholar educated in Literature and History at New York University, the University of Michigan, and Duquesne University. He has been an archivist at the Joint Archives of Holland at Hope College and at Carnegie Mellon University, and an educator at the Community College of Allegheny County (PA).